BUILDING
Vocabulary
Skills

Level 1
Student Edition

Columbus, OH • Chicago, IL • Redmond, WA

The **McGraw·Hill** Companies

www.sra4kids.com

 SRA

Send all inquiries to:
SRA/McGraw-Hill
8787 Orion Place
Columbus, OH 43240-4027

Printed in the United States of America.

ISBN 0-07-579612-0

5 6 7 8 9 QPD 07 06 05

The McGraw·Hill Companies

Table of Contents

Unit 1

Lesson 1: "Let's Read" Vocabulary 2
Word Meanings: Examples
Reference Skills: Alphabetical Order
Build New Vocabulary: More Than One
Word Play: Synonyms

Lesson 2: Vocabulary About Books 6
Word Meanings: Show the Meaning
Reference Skills: Alphabet Match
Build New Vocabulary: Compound Words
Word Play: Words in Words

Lesson 3: Vocabulary for Time 10
Word Meanings: Definitions
Reference Skills: Which Comes First?
Build New Vocabulary: Organizing Time
Word Play: Same or Different?

Lesson 4: "Family" Vocabulary 14
Word Meanings: Word Web
Reference Skills: Beginning Letters
Build New Vocabulary: Actions in the Past
Word Play: Yes or No?

Lesson 5: "Good" Vocabulary 18
Word Meanings: Demonstrate
Reference Skills: Dictionary Definitions
Build New Vocabulary: Context Clues
Word Play: Rhyming Words

Lesson 6: Vocabulary Review 22
Review Word Meanings: Let's Read

Unit 2

Lesson 7: Vocabulary for Animals 26
Word Meanings: Who Am I?
Reference Skills: Dictionary Definitions
Build New Vocabulary: Kinds of Animals
Word Play: Baby Animals

Lesson 8: "Folktales" Vocabulary 30
Word Meanings: Definitions
Reference Skills: Guide Words
Build New Vocabulary: Adding –er
Word Play: Matching Related Words

Lesson 9: The Circus 34
Word Meanings: Picture Definitions
Reference Skills: Dictionary Sentences
Build New Vocabulary: More Than One
Word Play: Grouping Words

Lesson 10: Vocabulary for Sounds 38
Word Meanings: Let's Hear It
Reference Skills: Dictionary Definitions
Build New Vocabulary: Adding –ing
Word Play: Nonsense Rhymes

Lesson 11: Vocabulary for Amounts 42
Word Meanings: Definitions
Reference Skills: Guide Words
Build New Vocabulary: Context Clues
Word Play: Word Search

Lesson 12: Vocabulary Review 46
Review Word Meanings: All About Animals

Unit 3

Lesson 13: "Things That Go" Vocabulary 50
Word Meanings: Picture Definitions
Reference Skills: Alphabetical Order
Build New Vocabulary: Compound Words
Word Play: Rhyming Words

Lesson 14: Our Neighborhood at Work ...54
Word Meanings: People and Places
Reference Skills: Dictionary Sentences
Build New Vocabulary: Base Words
Word Play: The Missing Vowels

Lesson 15: Places to Live 58
Word Meanings: Animal and People Homes
Reference Skills: Guide Words
Build New Vocabulary: Context Clues
Word Play: What Is It Made Of?

Lesson 16: Vocabulary for Making Faces .62
Word Meanings: Demonstrate
Reference Skills: Beginning, Middle, End
Build New Vocabulary: Adding –ing
Word Play: Related Words

Lesson 17: Describing People 66
Word Meanings: Synonyms
Reference Skills: How Many Syllables?
Build New Vocabulary: The Suffix –ful
Word Play: Animal Rhymes

Lesson 18: Vocabulary Review 70
Review Word Meanings: A Trip to Washington, D.C.

Unit 4

Lesson 19: "Weather" Vocabulary 74
Word Meanings: What's the Picture?
Reference Skills: Number of Syllables
Build New Vocabulary: Add –y
Word Play: Nonsense Rhymes

Lesson 20: Machines in Our Garden 78
Word Meanings: Picture Definitions
Reference Skills: More Than One Meaning
Build New Vocabulary: Words That Sound Alike
Word Play: Can You?

Lesson 21: "Earth" Vocabulary 82
Word Meanings: Definitions
Reference Skills: Alphabetical Order by Second Letter
Build New Vocabulary: Context Clues: Spanish Words
Word Play: Missing Consonants

Lesson 22: "Water" Vocabulary 86
Word Meanings: Answering Questions
Reference Skills: Dictionary Sentences
Build New Vocabulary: Compound Words
Word Play: Rhyming Words

Lesson 23: "Bad Behavior" Vocabulary 90
Word Meanings: Words That Mean the Same
Reference Skills: Glossary Sentences
Build New Vocabulary: Good and Bad
Word Play: Rhyming Clues

Lesson 24: Vocabulary Review 94
Review Word Meanings: What Kind of Weather

Unit 5

Lesson 25: "Journeys" Vocabulary 98
Word Meanings: Definitions
Reference Skills: More Than One Meaning
Build New Vocabulary: Irregular Past Tense
Word Play: Changing Letters

Lesson 26: "Keep Trying" Vocabulary 102
Word Meanings: Synonyms
Reference Skills: Which Comes First?
Build New Vocabulary: The Prefix *re–*
Word Play: How Many Words?

Lesson 27: "Shapes and Sizes" Vocabulary 106
Word Meanings: Picture Definitions
Reference Skills: Using a Glossary
Build New Vocabulary: Antonyms
Word Play: Similes

Lesson 28: Going to the Doctor's Office .. 110
Word Meanings: How Do You Feel?
Reference Skills: Which Is Correct?
Build New Vocabulary: Context Clues: Homophones
Word Play: Scrambled Words

Lesson 29: Prepositions 114
Word Meanings: Examples
Reference Skills: Alphabetize By Second Letter
Build New Vocabulary: *Up* and *Out*
Word Play: *A* or *Be?*

Lesson 30: Vocabulary Review 118
Review Word Meanings: Traveling to the Tournament

Unit 6

Lesson 31: "Being Afraid" Vocabulary .122
Word Meanings: Examples
Reference Skills: Dictionary Definitions
Build New Vocabulary: Compound Words
Word Play: Silly Rhymes

Lesson 32: More Animals 126
Word Meanings: Picture Definitions
Reference Skills: Guide Words
Build New Vocabulary: Animal Characteristics
Word Play: More Similes

Lesson 33: Parts of a House 130
Word Meanings: Describe It
Reference Skills: Alphabetical Order
Build New Vocabulary: Words That Go Together
Word Play: Things That Go Together

Lesson 34: "Movement" Vocabulary 134
Word Meanings: Demonstrate
Reference Skills: Glossary Sentences
Build New Vocabulary: Context Clues
Word Play: Crossword Puzzle

Lesson 35: Useful Objects 138
Word Meanings: Examples
Reference Skills: Dictionary Sentences
Build New Vocabulary: Useful Uses
Word Play: Rhymes

Lesson 36: Vocabulary Review 142
Review Word Meanings: A Frightful Tale

Cumulative Review 146

Strategies
Word Webs 150
Categorization 151
Linear Graphs 152
Context Clues 153
Word Relationships 155
Tools and Reference
Table of Contents ....T&R1
Words in Another Country ....T&R2

Prefixes and Suffixes ....T&R3
Base Words ....T&R4
Italian Words ....T&R5
Fun With Words ....T&R6
Dictionary Skills ....T&R7
Nouns, Verbs, and Adjectives ....T&R9
Glossary ....T&R10
Word Bank ....T&R29

"Let's Read" Vocabulary

1 **Word Meanings**

Examples

1. page   guess

2. page   finish

3. about   circle

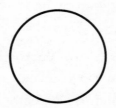

4. speak   ready

5. sentence   finish

6. circle   begin

Score _____
(Top Score 6)

Teacher Read each pair of words aloud. Have students cirlce the vocabulary word that matches the example picture.

Vocabulary	3. page	7. ready
List	4. about	8. circle
1. sentence	5. guess	9. speak
2. begin	6. finish	10. story

2 Reference Skills

Alphabetical Order

1.

2.

3.

4.

5.

Teacher Read each word aloud. Have students trace the first letter of each word. Point out that the words are in alphabetical order.

Score _____
(Top Score 5)

③ Build New Vocabulary

More Than One

1. circle**s**

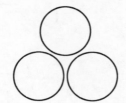

2. sentence**s**

3. picture**s**

4. page**s**

5. book**s**

6. artist**s**

Score _____
(Top Score 6)

Teacher Read the plural form of each word aloud. Have students trace the letter *s* at the end of each word to make the word plural.

Vocabulary List	3. page	7. ready
	4. about	8. circle
1. sentence	5. guess	9. speak
2. begin	6. finish	10. story

"Let's Read" Vocabulary • Build New Vocabulary

Word Play

Synonyms

1. begin

start

eat

2. finish

game

end

3. circle

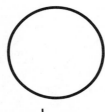

sphere

triangle

4. speak

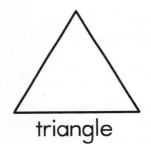

play

talk

5. story

radio

tale

Teacher Read each word aloud. Have students draw a circle around the word/picture combination that means the same as the vocabulary word.

Score _____
(Top Score 5)

Vocabulary About Books

①   Word Meanings

Show the Meaning

1. paper

   ○      ○      ○

2. ink

   ○      ○      ○

3. bookend

   ○      ○   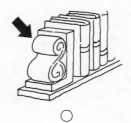   ○

4. study

   ○      ○      ○

5. backpack

   ○      ○      ○

Score _____
(Top Score 5)

Teacher Read each word aloud. Have students fill in the bubble below the picture that best matches the word.

Vocabulary List	3. due	7. borrow
1. study	4. backpack	8. return
2. bookend	5. ink	9. print
	6. fine	10. paper

 **Reference Skills**

Alphabet Match

1. borrow   b

2. return   d

3. due   f

4. fine   i

5. print   p

6. ink   r

Teacher Read each word aloud. Have students
draw a line from the word to its beginning letter.

Score _____
(Top Score 6)

3 Build New Vocabulary

Compound Words

1. bookstore

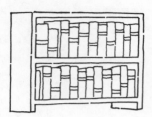

2. bookmark

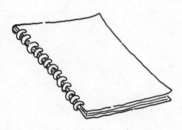

3. bookshelf

4. notebook

The Three Little Pigs

5. storybook

BOOKS GALORE

Score _____
(Top Score 5)

Teacher Read each word aloud. Have students draw a line from the word to the picture that best matches.

Vocabulary List	3. due	7. borrow
	4. backpack	8. return
1. study	5. ink	9. print
2. bookend	6. fine	10. paper

Vocabulary About Books • Build New Vocabulary

Words in Words

1. borrow

2. return

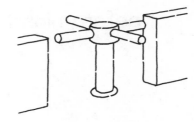

3. fine

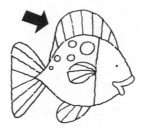

4. paper

5. print

Teacher Read each word aloud. Tell students to listen carefully to the hints and look at the pictures. Then have them circle each hidden word. Hints are in the *Teacher's Edition* on page 9.

Score _____
(Top Score 5)

Vocabulary for Time

① Word Meanings

Definitions

1. present
   - ○ going on now
   - ○ not ever happening

2. dawn
   - ○ just before nightfall
   - ○ the time when light appears in the morning

3. always
   - ○ at all times
   - ○ once in a while

4. past
   - ○ a time that has gone by
   - ○ at this minute

5. instant
   - ○ a very long amount of time
   - ○ a very short amount of time

6. daily
   - ○ every day
   - ○ once a week

Score _____
(Top Score 6)

Teacher Read each word and definition aloud. Have students fill in the bubble next to the correct definition of the word.

Vocabulary List		
1. present	3. daily	7. minute
2. instant	4. suddenly	8. always
	5. already	9. past
	6. sometime	10. dawn

Reference Skills

Which Comes First?

| a b c d e f g h i j k l m n o p q r s t u v w x y z |

1. daily always finish

2. dawn instant guess

3. present past minute

4. suddenly past sentence

5. sometime begin already

Teacher Read each set of words aloud. Tell students to look at each beginning letter. Have them draw a circle around the word that would come first in the dictionary.

Score _____
(Top Score 5)

❸ Build New Vocabulary

Organizing Time

1. second →  → hour

2. ____  → week →

   ____  → year

3. past → present → future

4. ____ day → weekly → monthy

Teacher Have students read each linear graph and then trace each missing word.

Vocabulary List	3. daily	7. minute
	4. suddenly	8. always
1. present	5. already	9. past
2. instant	6. sometime	10. dawn

Word Play

Same or Different?

1. past   present   S   D

2. always   sometime   S   D

3. dawn   morning   S   D

4. daily   suddenly   S   D

5. already   past   S   D

Teacher Read each pair of words aloud. Tell students to decide if the words have the same meaning or different meanings. Have them draw a circle around the *S* if the meanings are the same or around the *D* if the meanings are different.

Score _____
(Top Score 5)

"Family" Vocabulary

1 | **Word Meanings**

Word Web

grandmother

parent

cousin

swing set

FAMILY
MEMBERS

grandfather

house

aunt

car

Score _____
(Top Score 5)

Teacher Tell students to look at each picture in the word web. Have them draw a circle around the pictures that represent members of a family.

Vocabulary List		
1. belong	3. grandfather	7. support
2. parent	4. child	8. cousin
	5. members	9. related
	6. grandmother	10. depend

"Family" Vocabulary • **Word Meanings**

2 Reference Skills

Beginning Letters

1.

I belong to that family.

2.

My uncle's son is my cousin.

3.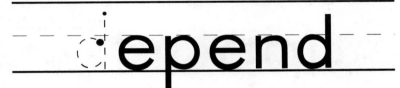

We depend on family to take care of us.

4.

There are five members in my family.

5.

To support someone is to help him or her.

Teacher Read each word and sentence aloud. Have students trace the beginning letter of each word. Help students notice that the words are in alphabetical order.

Score _____
(Top Score 5)

③ Build New Vocabulary

Actions in the Past

1. **belong**ed

2. **depend**ed

3. **support**ed

4. **borrow**ed

5. **return**ed

Teacher Read each word aloud. Have students trace the *-ed* suffix in each word.

Vocabulary List	3. grandfather	7. support
	4. child	8. cousin
1. belong	5. members	9. related
2. parent	6. grandmother	10. depend

"Family" Vocabulary • Build New Vocabulary

Word Play

Yes or No?

1. Is a child related to his or her grandmother?   Yes   No

2. Is a child older than his or her grandfather?   Yes   No

3. Can you depend on a baby to take care of you?   Yes   No

4. Can a cousin also be a parent?   Yes   No

5. Can a family member support another family member?   Yes   No

Teacher Read each question aloud. Have students draw a circle around *Yes* if the question answers something that is possible or a circle around *No* if the question answers something that is impossible.

Score _____
(Top Score 5)

"Good" Vocabulary

1 Word Meanings

Demonstrate

1. greet

 ○    ○

2. glad

 ○    ○

3. prize

 ○    ○

4. behave

 ○    ○

5. thank

 ○    ○

Score _____
(Top Score 5)

Teacher Read each word aloud. Have students fill in the bubble below the picture that best demonstrates the meaning of the word.

Vocabulary List		
1. behave	3. obey	7. deserve
2. thank	4. glad	8. promise
	5. prize	9. greet
	6. blessing	10. polite

② Reference Skills

Dictionary Definitions

1. greet
   ○ to be thankful   ○ to say hello

2. blessing
   ○ something that brings you happiness   ○ something that makes you sleepy

3. polite
   ○ unkind   ○ kind and thoughtful

4. deserve
   ○ to be worthy of; to earn   ○ to act properly

5. promise
   ○ to say good-bye   ○ to give your word that you will do something

Teacher Read each word and the definitions aloud. Have students fill in the bubble next to the correct definition of the word.

Score _____
(Top Score 5)

3 Build New Vocabulary

Context Clues

1. I made a _____ to my mom to clean my room, and I did it.
   promise   polite

2. We _____ our friends by saying, "Hello."
   greet   glad

3. I am _____ when my family eats together.
   behave   glad

4. We _____ people when they do something nice for us.
   thank   deserve

5. You might win a _____ at the fair.
   obey   prize

Score _____
(Top Score 5)

Teacher Tell students to listen carefully as you read each incomplete sentence aloud. Have them decide which word best completes the sentence and draw a circle around it.

Vocabulary List	3. obey	7. deserve
1. behave	4. glad	8. promise
2. thank	5. prize	9. greet
	6. blessing	10. polite

"Good" Vocabulary • Build New Vocabulary

Word Play

Rhyming Words

1. What word rhymes with *greet* and means "parts of the body on which a person stands or walks"?

_____
eet

2. What word rhymes with *glad* and means "angry"?

_____
ad

3. What word rhymes with *prize* and means "the bigness of something"?

_____
ize

4. What word rhymes with *thank* and means "a thing that holds money"?

_____
ank

Teacher Read each riddle aloud. Have students write in the correct beginning letter to answer each rhyming riddle.

Score _____
(Top Score 4)

Vocabulary Review

Review Word Meanings

1. The children sat in a <u>circle</u> for storytime.

○   ○   ○

2. I turned the <u>page</u> in the book.

○   ○   ○

3. She tried to <u>guess</u> the right answer.

○   ○   ○

4. She wanted to <u>speak</u> to the teacher.

○   ○   ○

5. He would only take a <u>minute</u> to tie his shoe.

○   ○   ○

Score _____
(Top Score 5)

Teacher Read aloud the story on page 22 in the *Teacher's Edition* OR read the sentences above for each number. Tell students to fill in the bubble below the picture that best matches the underlined word.

❷ Review Word Meanings

1. I like to <u>study</u> in my room.

 ○  ○  ○

2. He wrote me a letter on the <u>paper</u>.

 ○  ○  ○

3. She had to <u>return</u> the book.

 ○  ○  ○

4. Mario carries a blue-and-red <u>backpack</u>.

 ○  ○ 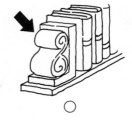 ○

5. I brush my teeth <u>daily</u>.

 ○  ○  ○

Teacher Read aloud the story on page 23 in the *Teacher's Edition* OR read the sentences above for each number. Tell students to fill in the bubble below the picture that best matches the underlined word.

Score _____
(Top Score 5)

③ Review Word Meanings

1. There are five <u>members</u> in my family.

 ○  ○  ○

2. My <u>grandmother</u> came to visit yesterday.

 ○  ○  ○

3. His <u>grandfather</u> takes him fishing.

 ○  ○  ○

4. The <u>child</u> played in the sand.

 ○  ○  ○

5. One day I hope to be a <u>parent</u>.

 ○  ○  ○

Score _____
(Top Score 5)

Teacher Read aloud the story on page 24 in the *Teacher's Edition* OR read the sentences above for each number. Tell students to fill in the bubble below the picture that best matches the underlined word.

4 Review Word Meanings

1. <u>Dawn</u> is my favorite time of day.

 ○    ○    ○

2. I was <u>glad</u> to return home.

 ○    ○    ○

3. She received a <u>prize</u> for the best drawing.

 ○    ○    ○

4. I like to <u>greet</u> my dad at the bus stop.

 ○    ○    ○

5. I wrote a letter to <u>thank</u> Jean for the gift.

 ○    ○    ○

Teacher Read aloud the story on page 25 in the *Teacher's Edition* OR read the sentences above for each number. Tell students to fill in the bubble below the picture that best matches the underlined word.

Score
(Top Score 5)

Vocabulary for Animals

1 Word Meanings

Who Am I?

1. bee

A.

2. bird

B.

3. cat

C.

4. cow

D.

5. duck

E.

6. dog

F.

7. fish

G.

8. fly

H.

9. frog

I.

10. horse

J.

Score _____
(Top Score 10)

Teacher Read each word aloud. Have students draw a line from the vocabulary word to its matching picture.

Vocabulary List		
1. cat	3. horse	7. bee
2. dog	4. duck	8. fish
	5. fly	9. frog
	6. bird	10. cow

2 Reference Skills

Dictionary Definitions

1. A **bee** makes honey.

A.

2. A **cat** has fur.

B.

3. A **duck** has wings.

C.

4. A **cow** gives milk.

D.

5. A **dog** can bark.

E.

Teacher Read each definition sentence aloud. Have students draw a line from the sentence to its matching picture.

Score _____
(Top Score 5)

Vocabulary for Animals • Reference Skills

3 Build New Vocabulary

Kinds of Animals

1. dog

2. cat

3. fish

4. bird

5. duck

Score _____
(Top Score 5)

Teacher Read each word aloud. Have students draw an X over the picture that does NOT belong.

Vocabulary List	3. horse	7. bee
	4. duck	8. fish
1. cat	5. fly	9. frog
2. dog	6. bird	10. cow

Vocabulary for Animals • Build New Vocabulary

Word Play

Baby Animals

1. sheep

A. kitten

2. cat

B. foal

3. cow

C. lamb

4. dog

D. pup

5. horse

E. calf

Teacher Read each word aloud. Have students draw a line from the animal name to the picture of its young.

Score _____
(Top Score 5)

"Folktales" Vocabulary

1   **Word Meanings**

Definitions

1. mouth

A. a pleasing combination of sounds

2. music

B. a story

3. north

C. people

4. tale

D. opposite of south

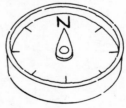

5. folks

E. part of the body that contains a tongue, teeth, and gums

Score _____
(Top Score 5)

Teacher Read each word aloud. Have students draw a line from the vocabulary word to its matching picture and definition.

Vocabulary List	3. music	7. mouth
1. east	4. live	8. tale
2. west	5. south	9. folks
	6. north	10. singer

Reference Skills

Guide Words

1. drop   good
   - ○ east
   - ○ west

2. lion   pat
   - ○ north
   - ○ tale

3. quiet   tame
   - ○ folks
   - ○ singer

4. minute   past
   - ○ east
   - ○ mouth

5. thank   win
   - ○ west
   - ○ music

6. rich   violet
   - ○ singer
   - ○ west

7. lemon   mop
   - ○ live
   - ○ mouth

8. snail   trim
   - ○ singer
   - ○ tale

9. until   yellow
   - ○ south
   - ○ west

10. eye   found
    - ○ east
    - ○ folks

Teacher Read each pair of guide words aloud. Have students fill in the bubble next to the word that would appear between the two guide words.

Score _____
(Top Score 10)

③ Build New Vocabulary

Adding -er

1. teacher

2. reader

3. thinker

4. painter

5. player

Score _____
(Top Score 5)

Teacher Read each word aloud. Have students trace the -er ending in each word.

Vocabulary List		
1. east	3. music	7. mouth
2. west	4. live	8. tale
	5. south	9. folks
	6. north	10. singer

"Folktales" Vocabulary • Build New Vocabulary

 **Word Play**

Matching Related Words

1. live	**A.** thought
2. see	**B.** tale
3. sing	**C.** life
4. tell	**D.** sight
5. think	**E.** song

Teacher Read each word aloud. Have students draw a line from the word to its related word on the right.

Score _____
(Top Score 5)

The Circus

Picture Definitions

1. clown

2. elephant

3. lion

4. tiger

5. tent

Score _____
(Top Score 5)

Teacher Read each word aloud. Have students fill in the bubble below the picture that matches the word.

Vocabulary List	3. lion	7. crowd
1. tame	4. tent	8. hoop
2. clown	5. elephant	9. ticket
	6. tiger	10. show

Reference Skills

Dictionary Sentences

1. A **lion** can roar.

A.

2. You need a **ticket** to see the show.

B.

3. The **clown** did funny tricks.

C.

4. A **tiger** is a big cat.

D.

5. The biggest land animal is an **elephant.**

E.

Teacher Read each sentence aloud. Have students draw a line from the sentence to its matching picture.

Score _____
(Top Score 5)

More Than One

At the circus,

I saw two

elephants, three

tame lions, four

clowns, five tents,

and six tickets.

Now I have been

to two shows.

Score _____
(Top Score 6)

Teacher Read each sentence aloud. Have students trace the -s in each sentence.

Vocabulary List	3. lion	7. crowd
	4. tent	8. hoop
1. tame	5. elephant	9. ticket
2. clown	6. tiger	10. show

Word Play

Grouping Words

1. hoop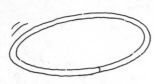

2. clown

People

3. ticket

4. lion

5. crowd

Things

6. tiger

7. tent

Animals

8. elephant

Teacher Have students draw a line from the
picture on the left to the word it can be
categorized with on the right.

Score _____
(Top Score 8)

Vocabulary for Sounds

1 Word Meanings

Let's Hear It

1. chirp

A.

2. croak

B.

3. roar

C.

4. squeal

D.

5. quack

E.

Score _____
(Top Score 5)

Teacher Read each word aloud. Have students draw a line from the word to the animal that makes the sound.

Vocabulary List		
1. quack	3. chirp	7. hum
2. squeal	4. groan	8. roar
	5. chatter	9. giggle
	6. whisper	10. croak

Vocabulary for Sounds • Word Meanings

Reference Skills

Dictionary Definitions

1. to talk quietly
   - ○ whisper
   - ○ squeal

2. a silly laugh
   - ○ croak
   - ○ giggle

3. a deep, sad sound
   - ○ groan
   - ○ chatter

4. to sing with a closed mouth
   - ○ hum
   - ○ chirp

5. fast, silly talk
   - ○ quack
   - ○ chatter

6. flat sound a duck makes
   - ○ chirp
   - ○ quack

7. a loud, deep sound
   - ○ whisper
   - ○ roar

8. deep, grating sound a frog makes
   - ○ squeal
   - ○ croak

9. a short, sharp sound
   - ○ roar
   - ○ chirp

10. a loud, high-pitched cry
    - ○ squeal
    - ○ hum

Teacher Read each definition aloud. Have students fill in the bubble of the word that matches the definition.

Score _____
(Top Score 10)

③ Build New Vocabulary

Adding *-ing*

1. The lion is roaring.

2. The pig is squealing.

3. The birds are chirping.

4. The frog is croaking.

5. The ducks are quacking.

Score _____
(Top Score 5)

Teacher Read each sentence aloud. Have students trace the *-ing* ending in each sentence.

Vocabulary List	3. chirp	7. hum
	4. groan	8. roar
1. quack	5. chatter	9. giggle
2. squeal	6. whisper	10. croak

Vocabulary for Sounds • Build New Vocabulary

Word Play

Nonsense Rhymes

1. An eel does not _____ when it steals a meal.
   - ○ squeal
   - ○ croak

2. My thumb went numb, so I started to _____ .
   - ○ hum
   - ○ giggle

3. Do you moan and _____ when you pick up a stone?
   - ○ chirp
   - ○ groan

4. The floor at the store makes a snore and a _____ .
   - ○ roar
   - ○ croak

5. "Egg yolks make me choke," I spoke with a _____ .
   - ○ groan
   - ○ croak

Teacher Read each nonsense rhyme aloud. Have students fill in the bubble next to the word that completes the nonsense rhyme.

Score _____
(Top Score 5)

Vocabulary for Amounts

 Word Meanings

Definitions

1. **batch:** an amount baked at one time; a group

2. **bundle:** a number of things tied or bound together

3. **dozen:** a group of twelve

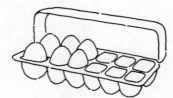 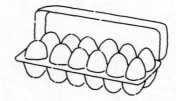

4. **equal:** the same in size or number

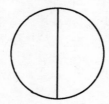 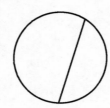

5. **double:** two of the same thing

Score _____
(Top Score 5)

Teacher Read each word and definition aloud. Have students draw a circle around the picture that best matches the word and definition.

Vocabulary List	3. heap	7. double
1. equal	4. batch	8. bunch
2. bundle	5. dozen	9. enough
	6. exact	10. bushel

Reference Skills

Guide Words

1. baby   crow
   - ○ batch
   - ○ heap

2. day   dream
   - ○ equal
   - ○ dozen

3. end   fly
   - ○ bunch
   - ○ enough

4. hay   ink
   - ○ heap
   - ○ bundle

5. date   draw
   - ○ exact
   - ○ double

6. broad   butter
   - ○ heap
   - ○ bushel

7. age   canary
   - ○ bunch
   - ○ exact

8. dirt   evening
   - ○ equal
   - ○ batch

9. draw   flower
   - ○ bushel
   - ○ exact

10. bread   dog
    - ○ bundle
    - ○ enough

Teacher Read each pair of guide words aloud. Have students fill in the bubble next to the word that would appear between the two guide words.

Score _____
(Top Score 10)

Vocabulary for Amounts • Reference Skills

3 Build New Vocabulary

Context Clues

1. a _____ eggs
   ○ double   ○ dozen

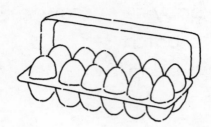

2. a _____ of biscuits
   ○ bushel   ○ batch

3. a _____ of apples
   ○ exact   ○ bushel

4. a _____ of newspapers
   ○ bundle   ○ enough

5. a _____ of bananas
   ○ bunch   ○ heap

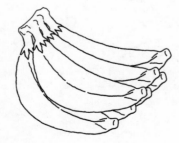

Score _____
(Top Score 5)

Teacher Read each phrase aloud. Have students fill in the bubble next to the word that best completes the phrase.

Vocabulary List	3. heap	7. double
1. equal	4. batch	8. bunch
2. bundle	5. dozen	9. enough
	6. exact	10. bushel

Vocabulary for Amounts • Build New Vocabulary

Word Play

Word Search

batch		bunch		bundle
bushel	double		dozen	enough
equal		exact	heap	

b	a	b	u	n	d	l	e	e	d	e	l	e
u	e	a	d	d	o	u	b	n	e	q	e	b
l	x	t	u	o	z	e	u	o	x	u	l	u
c	c	c	n	h	e	a	p	u	a	a	l	n
b	u	h	e	e	n	e	x	g	c	l	e	c
u	b	u	s	h	e	l	d	h	t	l	d	h
l	e	b	e	d	o	u	b	l	e	z	l	e
x	q	o	o	n	h	e	s	z	e	c	h	l

Teacher Have students complete the word search by drawing a circle around each vocabulary word from the word box. Remind them that words are found going across and going down.

Score _____
(Top Score 10)

Vocabulary Review

1 **Review Word Meanings**

1. The <u>cow</u> ate grass in the field.

2. The <u>horse</u> trotted into the barn.

3. The <u>frog</u> hopped into the pond.

4. The <u>duck</u> quickly swam to the shore.

5. The <u>fish</u> would not swim near the hook.

Score _____
(Top Score 5)

Teacher Read aloud the story on page 46 in the *Teacher's Edition* OR read the sentences above for each number. Tell students to fill in the bubble below the picture that best matches the underlined word.

② Review Word Meanings

1. We set up our <u>tent</u> away from the campfire.

 ○    ○    ○

2. I bought a <u>ticket</u> to the circus.

 ○    ○    ○

3. The <u>clown</u> had a big red nose.

 ○    ○    ○

4. The <u>elephant</u> ate the whole bucket of peanuts.

 ○    ○    ○

5. The lion roared as he jumped through the <u>hoop</u>.

 ○    ○   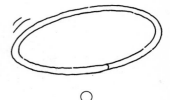 ○

Teacher Read aloud the story on page 47 in the *Teacher's Edition* OR read the sentences above for each number. Tell students to fill in the bubble below the picture that best matches the underlined word.

Score _____
(Top Score 5)

3 Review Word Meanings

1. I could hear the bird <u>chirp</u> in the tree.

    ○   ○   ○

2. The frog let out a <u>croak</u> after he ate the fly.

    ○   ○   ○

3. When the ducks wanted more corn, they would <u>quack</u>.

    ○   ○   ○

4. We heard a loud <u>squeal</u> from the pigpen.

    ○   ○   ○

5. From behind the chair, Mother could hear a <u>giggle</u>.

    ○   ○   ○

Score _____
(Top Score 5)

Teacher Read aloud the story on page 48 in the *Teacher's Edition* OR read the sentences above for each number. Tell students to fill in the bubble below the picture that best matches the underlined word.

Review Word Meanings

1. The grocer ordered a <u>bushel</u> of apples.

2. Aunt Maria sold her <u>batch</u> of biscuits at the bake sale.

3. Every Sunday Uncle Jack would buy a <u>dozen</u> roses.

4. The farmer gathered a <u>heap</u> of grain.

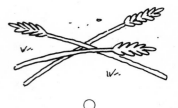

5. The boys gathered a <u>bundle</u> of sticks for the campfire.

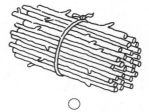

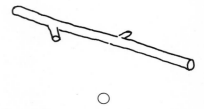

Teacher Read aloud the story on page 49 in the *Teacher's Edition* OR read the sentences above for each number. Tell students to fill in the bubble below the picture that best matches the underlined word.

Score _____
(Top Score 5)

"Things That Go" Vocabulary

1 Word Meanings

Picture Definitions

1. canoe

A.

2. train

B.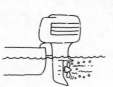

3. airplane

C.

4. motor

D.

5. carriage

E.

6. bicycle

F.

7. scooter

G.

8. tractor

H.

Score _____
(Top Score 8)

Teacher Read each word aloud. Have students draw a line from the vocabulary word on the left to the picture it matches on the right.

Vocabulary List		
1. bicycle	3. canoe	7. train
2. skateboard	4. tractor	8. airplane
	5. cart	9. scooter
	6. motor	10. carriage

Alphabetical Order

_____ _____ scooter

_____ _____ skateboard

_____ _____ airplane

_____ _____ train

_____ _____ bicycle

_____ _____ motor

Teacher Read each word aloud. Using the numbers 1–6, have students place the words in alphabetical order by placing a 1 next to the word that would come first, 2 next to the word that would come second, and so on.

Score _____
(Top Score 6)

"Things That Go" Vocabulary • Reference Skills

3 Build New Vocabulary

Compound Words

1. _____
mail box

321 Oak Street

2. _____
air plane

3. _____
skate board

4. _____
side walk

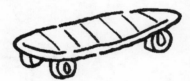

5. _____
sail boat

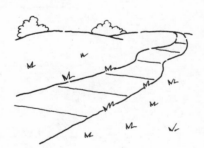

Score _____
(Top Score 5)

Teacher Read each word aloud. Have students trace the smaller word to make the compound word that matches the picture.

Vocabulary List	3. canoe	7. train
1. bicycle	4. tractor	8. airplane
2. skateboard	5. cart	9. scooter
	6. motor	10. carriage

"Things That Go" Vocabulary • Build New Vocabulary

Word Play

Rhyming Words

train

track	bank	rain
cane	date	plane

- -

cart

pin	dart	tan
part	heart	ran

Teacher Read each word aloud. Have students draw a circle around the words that rhyme with the words *train* and *cart*.

Score _____
(Top Score 6)

Our Neighborhood at Work

1 **Word Meanings**

People and Places

1. building

2. operator

People

3. lifeguard

4. factory

Places

5. plumber

6. clerk

Score _____
(Top Score 6)

Teacher Read each word aloud. Have students draw a line from the picture of the vocabulary word to the correct category.

Vocabulary List	3. clerk	7. uniform
	4. factory	8. operator
1. building	5. handmade	9. plumber
2. police	6. office	10. lifeguard

Our Neighborhood at Work • Word Meanings

Reference Skills

Dictionary Sentences

1. A **clerk** works in a store.

A.

2. Goods are made in a **factory.**

B.

3. A **plumber** fixes water pipes.

C.

4. An **office** is a room to work in.

D.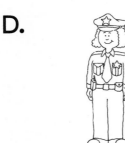

5. The policewoman wears a **uniform** when she is on duty.

E.

Teacher Read each sentence aloud. Have students draw a line from the sentence to the picture it matches.

Score _____
(Top Score 5)

❸ Build New Vocabulary

Base Words

1.

2.

3.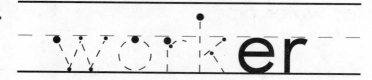

4.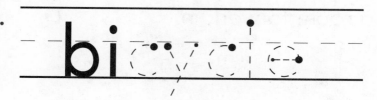

5.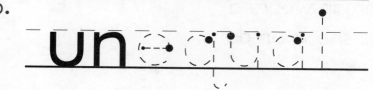

Score _____
(Top Score 5)

Teacher Have students trace the base word in each word.

Vocabulary List	3. clerk	7. uniform
1. building	4. factory	8. operator
2. police	5. handmade	9. plumber
	6. office	10. lifeguard

Our Neighborhood at Work • Build New Vocabulary

Word Play

The Missing Vowels

building	lifeguard	clerk	factory
handmade	office	operator	plumber
police	uniform		

1. b _ _ ld _ ng

2. l _ f _ g _ _ rd

3. _ p _ r _ t _ r

4. pl _ mb _ r

5. h _ ndm _ d _

Teacher Read each word in the box aloud.
Have the students write in the missing vowels
in each word.

Score _____
(Top Score 16)

Places to Live

(1)   Word Meanings

Animal and People Homes

1. cabin   cage

2. cave   cottage

3. coop   wigwam

4. hut   den

5. igloo   nest

Score _____
(Top Score 5)

Teacher Read each pair of words aloud. Have students look at each pair of pictures and then circle the word that represents where people live.

Vocabulary List		
	3. wigwam	7. igloo
	4. coop	8. cottage
1. nest	5. hut	9. cave
2. cabin	6. den	10. cage

Places to Live • Word Meanings

2 Reference Skills

Guide Words

1. cabin
   ○ bank/early   ○ glad/jump

2. cage
   ○ bank/early   ○ glad/jump

3. hut
   ○ bank/early   ○ glad/jump

4. den
   ○ bank/early   ○ glad/jump

5. igloo
   ○ bank/early   ○ glad/jump

Teacher Read each word aloud. Have students fill in the bubble next to the set of guide words each vocabulary word would be found between.

Score _____
(Top Score 5)

Build New Vocabulary

Context Clues

1. We paddled the **canoe** down the river.

A.

2. Although it was made of ice, the **igloo** was warm inside.

B.

3. We wore **moccasins** on our feet.

C.

4. A **raccoon** has mask-like markings on its face and a bushy, ringed tail.

D.

5. We picked the **tomato** from the plant.

E.
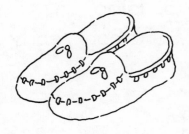

Score _____
(Top Score 5)

Teacher Read each sentence aloud. Have students draw a line from the sentence to the picture it matches.

Vocabulary List	3. wigwam	7. igloo
	4. coop	8. cottage
1. nest	5. hut	9. cave
2. cabin	6. den	10. cage

Places to Live • Build New Vocabulary

Word Play

What Is It Made Of?

1. cabin

A. ice

2. cage

B. twigs and leaves

3. hut

C. thatch

4. igloo

D. wire

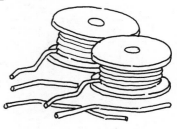

5. nest

E. wood

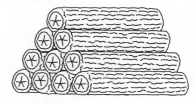

Teacher Read each word aloud. Have students draw a line from the word to the picture of the material usually used to build that home. Have students refer to the pictures on page 58 for help.

Score _____
(Top Score 5)

Vocabulary for Making Faces

1 **Word Meanings**

Demonstrate

1. grin

A.

2. frown

B.

3. mask

C.

4. wink

D.

5. yawn

E.

Score _____
(Top Score 5)

Teacher Read each word aloud. Have students draw a line from the word to the picture it matches.

Vocabulary List	3. smile	7. blink
	4. blush	8. surprise
1. mask	5. yawn	9. pretend
2. frown	6. wink	10. grin

Vocabulary for Making Faces • Word Meanings

Reference Skills

Beginning, Middle, End

1. blush
   - ○ A–H   ○ I–Q   ○ R–Z

2. pretend
   - ○ A–H   ○ I–Q   ○ R–Z

3. mask
   - ○ A–H   ○ I–Q   ○ R–Z

4. wink
   - ○ A–H   ○ I–Q   ○ R–Z

5. frown
   - ○ A–H   ○ I–Q   ○ R–Z

6. surprise
   - ○ A–H   ○ I–Q   ○ R–Z

Teacher Read each word aloud. Have students fill in the bubble next to the letters that tell where the word can be found in a dictionary.

Score _____
(Top Score 6)

3 Build New Vocabulary

Add -ing

1. Why do you keep blink_____ing_____ your eyes?

2. I am blush_____ing_____ because I am shy.

3. Luis is frown_____ing_____ in that picture.

4. Tora is pretend_____ing_____ to be sad.

5. My doll looks as if she is wink_____ing_____ at me.

6. Josh cannot stop yawn_____ing_____ today.

Score _____
(Top Score 6)

Teacher Read each sentence aloud. Have students trace the *-ing* at the end of the vocabulary words.

Vocabulary List	3. smile	7. blink
1. mask	4. blush	8. surprise
2. frown	5. yawn	9. pretend
	6. wink	10. grin

Vocabulary for Making Faces • Build New Vocabulary

 **Word Play**

Related Words

1. grin
   - ○ smile
   - ○ frown

2. wink
   - ○ blush
   - ○ blink

3. mask
   - ○ pretend
   - ○ yawn

4. yawn
   - ○ wink
   - ○ sleepy

5. giggle
   - ○ laugh
   - ○ blink

6. blush
   - ○ red
   - ○ blue

7. surprise
   - ○ slowly
   - ○ suddenly

8. frown
   - ○ joyful
   - ○ unhappy

Teacher Read each word aloud. Have students fill in the bubble next to the word that best relates to the vocabulary word.

Score _____
(Top Score 8)

Describing People

Word Meanings

Synonyms

1. silly   mad   angry

2. beautiful   handsome   ugly

3. shy   truthful   honest

4. angry   silly   funny

5. sleepy   lucky   drowsy

6. pretty   beautiful   gentle

Score _____
(Top Score 6)

Teacher Read each word aloud. Have students draw an X over the word that is NOT a synonym.

Vocabulary List	3. gentle	7. handsome
	4. drowsy	8. honest
1. shy	5. silly	9. angry
2. beautiful	6. lucky	10. nice

Describing People • Word Meanings

2 Reference Skills

How Many Syllables?

1. _____ angry

2. _____ beautiful

3. _____ honest

4. _____ gentle

5. _____ nice

Teacher Read each word aloud. Count the number of syllables in each word with the students. Then have the students write the number on the line provided.

Score _____
(Top Score 5)

3 Build New Vocabulary

The Suffix -ful

1. The meadow was beauti_____.

2. Pedro was very help_____.

3. The kittens are play_____.

4. It was a rest_____ afternoon.

5. Leo is care_____ when he is

crossing the street.

Score _____
(Top Score 5)

Teacher Have students trace the -ful at the end of the vocabulary words to make the sentence match the picture.

Vocabulary List	3. gentle	7. handsome
1. shy	4. drowsy	8. honest
2. beautiful	5. silly	9. angry
	6. lucky	10. nice

Describing People • Build New Vocabulary

 **Word Play**

Animal Rhymes

1. shy

A.

2. nice

B.

3. slow

C.

4. fake

D.

5. that

E.

Teacher Read each word aloud. Have students draw a line from the word to the picture of the animal that it rhymes with.

Score _____
(Top Score 5)

Vocabulary Review

1   **Review Word Meanings**

1. The <u>airplane</u> flew from New York to Texas.

      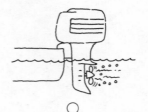

2. Luisa pedaled the <u>bicycle</u> up the hill.

3. The <u>train</u> chugged slowly up the mountain.

4. Mom and I paddled the <u>canoe</u> down the river.

5. The farmer plowed the field with the <u>tractor</u>.

Score _____
(Top Score 5)

Teacher Read aloud the story on page 70 in the *Teacher's Edition* OR read the sentences for each number. Tell students to fill in the bubble below the picture that best matches the underlined word.

Vocabulary Review

② Review Word Meanings

1. We watched the people make cars at the <u>factory</u>.

 ○    ○    ○

2. Uncle Martin wears a tie when he works in the <u>office</u>.

 ○    ○    ○

3. The <u>police</u> officer gave us directions to the park.

 ○    ○    ○

4. The <u>operator</u> wore her safety goggles.

 ○    ○    ○

5. The <u>plumber</u> used his wrench to fix the pipe.

 ○    ○    ○

Teacher Read aloud the story on page 71 in the *Teacher's Edition* OR read the sentences for each number. Tell students to fill in the bubble below the picture that best matches the underlined word.

Score _____
(Top Score 5)

Vocabulary Review

Review Word Meanings

1. Soto used bark and leaves to build the <u>wigwam</u>.

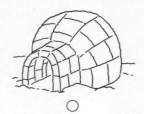   ○      ○      ○

2. The family huddled together inside the <u>igloo</u>.

   ○   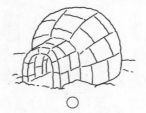   ○      ○

3. Mother told us to come into the <u>hut</u> to get away from the hot sun.

   ○   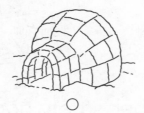   ○      ○

4. The bat rested in the <u>cave</u> during the day.

   ○      ○      ○

5. The bluebird brought food back to her <u>nest</u>.

   ○      ○      ○

Score _____
(Top Score 5)

Teacher Read aloud the story on page 72 in the *Teacher's Edition* OR read the sentences for each number. Tell students to fill in the bubble below the picture that best matches the underlined word.

Vocabulary Review

4 Review Word Meanings

1. Would you <u>frown</u> at a clown?

 ○    ○    ○

2. Peter was <u>angry</u> that he had to wait for his turn.

 ○    ○    ○

3. Talking in front of a lot of people always makes me <u>blush</u>.

 ○    ○    ○

4. We all laughed at the <u>silly</u> clowns.

 ○    ○    ○

5. The cat was <u>lucky</u> that the firefighter rescued it.

 ○    ○    ○

Teacher Read aloud the story on page 73 in the *Teacher's Edition* OR read the sentences for each number. Tell students to fill in the bubble below the picture that best matches the underlined word.

Score _____
(Top Score 5)

Vocabulary Review

"Weather" Vocabulary

① Word Meanings

What's the Picture?

1. cloud

A.

2. frost

B.

3. rainbow

C.

4. sunny

D.

5. tornado

E.

6. snowfall

F.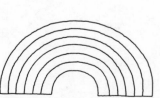

Score _____
(Top Score 6)

Teacher Read each word aloud. Have students draw a line from the vocabulary word on the left to its matching picture on the right.

Vocabulary List	3. sunny	7. rainbow
1. rain	4. cloud	8. tornado
2. frost	5. fog	9. snowfall
	6. hurricane	10. thunder

"Weather" Vocabulary • Word Meanings

② Reference Skills

Number of Syllables

1. _____ sunny

2. _____ rain

3. _____ thunder

4. _____ hurricane

5. _____ fog

6. _____ tornado

Teacher Have students count the number of syllables in each word. Tell them to write the number in the space provided.

Score _____
(Top Score 6)

3 Build New Vocabulary

Add -y

1. rain + y = _____

2. frost + y = _____

3. sun + n + y = _____

4. cloud + y = _____

5. snow + y = _____

Score _____
(Top Score 5)

Teacher Have students look at each equation. Instruct them to write the word on the line, adding -y to the letters as indicated.

Vocabulary List	3. sunny	7. rainbow
	4. cloud	8. tornado
1. rain	5. fog	9. snowfall
2. frost	6. hurricane	10. thunder

"Weather" Vocabulary • Build New Vocabulary

4 Word Play

Nonsense Rhymes

| rain | tornado | sunny | fog |

1. A <u>frog</u> left its <u>log</u> to <u>jog</u> in the _____ .

2. On the way to <u>Spain</u>, I saw _____ in the <u>plane</u>.

3. The <u>funny</u> bee makes <u>honey</u> only when it is _____ _____ .

4. A _____ ! Oh, <u>no</u>! It will <u>blow</u> things that <u>grow</u>!

Teacher Read aloud each rhyme. Have students write the word from the box that completes it. The underlined words rhyme with the answer.

Score _____
(Top Score 4)

Machines in Our Garden

1 **Word Meanings**

Picture Definitions

ax	hole	seed	shovel	weed

1. _____

2. _____

3. _____

4. _____

5. _____

Score _____
(Top Score 5)

Teacher Have students look at each picture and write the word from the box that matches on the line provided.

Vocabulary List	3. ax	7. seed
1. shovel	4. plow	8. hole
2. wheelbarrow	5. weed	9. field
	6. soil	10. fill

 **Reference Skills**

More Than One Meaning

1. plow

 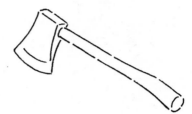 

2. shovel

 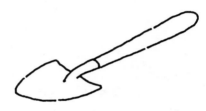 

3. weed

4. field

  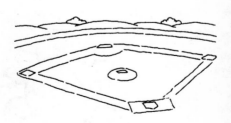

Teacher Read each word aloud. Have students draw an X over the picture that does not match the meaning of the word.

Score _____
(Top Score 4)

3 Build New Vocabulary

Words That Sound Alike

1.  ○ hole ○ whole

2.  ○ ate ○ eight

3. 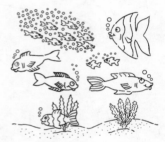 ○ sea ○ see

4.  ○ tale ○ tail

5.  ○ son ○ sun

Score _____
(Top Score 5)

Teacher Read each word choice aloud. Have students darken the oval next to the word that matches the picture.

Vocabulary List		
	3. ax	7. seed
	4. plow	8. hole
1. shovel	5. weed	9. field
2. wheelbarrow	6. soil	10. fill

Machines in Our Garden • Build New Vocabulary

Word Play

Can You?

1. Can a farmer plow a field?

2. Can soil shovel an ax?

3. Can you put a seed in a hole?

4. Can an ax shovel a wheelbarrow?

5. Can you fill a hole?

6. Can a gardener pull a weed from the soil?

Teacher Read each question aloud. Have students write the word *yes* or *no* to answer the question correctly.

Score _____
(Top Score 6)

"Earth" Vocabulary

   **Word Meanings**

Definitions

ash	cliff	forest	island	tip

1. _____

- - - - - - - - - - - - - - - - - -

_____

the end point of something

2. _____

- - - - - - - - - - - - - - - - - -

_____

a small area of land surrounded by water

3. _____

- - - - - - - - - - - - - - - - - -

_____

gray powder left by something that has been burned

4. _____

- - - - - - - - - - - - - - - - - -

_____

an area of land covered with trees and other plants

5. _____

- - - - - - - - - - - - - - - - - -

_____

a high, steep wall of rock

Score _____
(Top Score 5)

Teacher Read each definition aloud. Have students write the word from the box that matches the definition.

Vocabulary List	3. forest	7. prairie
1. ash	4. cliff	8. tip
2. canyon	5. island	9. valley
	6. nature	10. mountain

"Earth" Vocabulary • Word Meanings

2 Reference Skills

Alphabetical Order by Second Letter

1. _____ fruit   _____ forest

2. _____ plant   _____ prairie

3. _____ nest   _____ nature

4. _____ volcano   _____ valley

5. _____ cliff   _____ canyon

Teacher Read each set of words aloud. Have students write *1* next to the word that would come first in alphabetical order and *2* next to the word that would come next.

Score _____
(Top Score 5)

3 Build New Vocabulary

Context Clues: Spanish Words

1. I like to eat a crunchy <u>taco</u>.

2. They sat on the <u>patio</u> and enjoyed the sun.

3. We rode a donkey into the deep <u>canyon</u>.

4. The <u>alligator</u> came out of the water to rest.

5. The <u>mosquito</u> landed on my arm.

Score _____
(Top Score 5)

Teacher Read each sentence aloud. Have students draw a line from the sentence to the picture that matches the underlined word.

Vocabulary List		
1. ash	3. forest	7. prairie
2. canyon	4. cliff	8. tip
	5. island	9. valley
	6. nature	10. mountain

"Earth" Vocabulary • Build New Vocabulary

Missing Consonants

ash	forest	island	mountain	nature

1.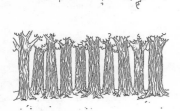

 __ o __ e __ __

2.

 __ __ o u __ __ __ a i __

3.

 i __ __ __ a __ __ __

4.

 __ a __ u __ e

5.

 a __ __ __

Teacher Have students look at each picture and provide the missing consonants for each word. Have students use the words in the box for reference.

Score _____
(Top Score 17)

"Water" Vocabulary

1 **Word Meanings**

Answering Questions

1. Can you fill a glass with a drop   yes   no
   of dew?

2. If your toy boat has a leak,   yes   no
   will it still float?

3. If a river is overflowing, is it   smaller   larger
   getting smaller or larger?

4. Can a whale live in a   yes   no
   puddle?

5. Which is larger—a lake or   lake   ocean
   an ocean?

Score _____
(Top Score 5)

Teacher Read each question
and the two answer choices
aloud. Have students circle the
correct answer.

Vocabulary List	3. lake	7. float
	4. ice	8. hose
1. river	5. puddle	9. leak
2. ocean	6. dew	10. overflow

Reference Skills

Dictionary Sentences

1. Drops of <u>dew</u> form on flowers.

2. Turn on the <u>hose</u> and water the garden.

3. A raft is used to <u>float</u> on water.

4. Evan splashed in the <u>puddle</u>.

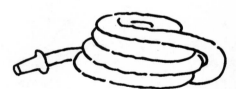

5. <u>Ice</u> is frozen water.

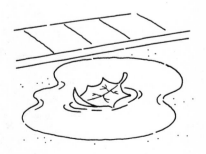

Teacher Read each sentence aloud. Have students draw a line from the dictionary sentence to the picture that best represents the underlined word.

Score _____
(Top Score 5)

3 Build New Vocabulary

Compound Words

1. ice water

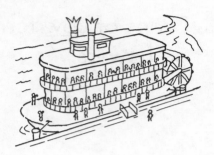

2. dewdrop

3. riverboat

4. riverside

Score _____
(Top Score 4)

Teacher Read each word aloud. Have students draw a line from the compound word to the picture that matches.

Vocabulary List	3. lake	7. float
	4. ice	8. hose
1. river	5. puddle	9. leak
2. ocean	6. dew	10. overflow

"Water" Vocabulary • Build New Vocabulary

Word Play

Rhyming Words

1. I would think <u>twice</u> about chewing on

_____

_ _ _ _ _ _ _ _ _ _ _ _ _ _ _ _ _

_____ .

2. The lettuce <u>grows</u> if you water it with the

_____

_ _ _ _ _ _ _ _ _ _ _ _ _ _ _ _ _

_____ .

3. Claire made the <u>mistake</u> of taking her <u>snake</u> to the

_____

_ _ _ _ _ _ _ _ _ _ _ _ _ _ _ _ _

_____ .

4. Our coach asked us to <u>huddle</u> next to the

_____

_ _ _ _ _ _ _ _ _ _ _ _ _ _ _ _ _

_____ .

5. Did you <u>sneak</u> a <u>peak</u> at the

_____

_ _ _ _ _ _ _ _ _ _ _ _ _ _ _ _ _

_____ ?

Teacher Read each sentence aloud. Have students write the vocabulary word that rhymes with each underlined word. Have students refer to vocabulary words that are displayed in the classroom.

Score _____
(Top Score 5)

"Bad Behavior" Vocabulary

1 **Word Meanings**

Words That Mean the Same

grab	greedy	nasty	slap	tease

1. **snatch:** to grasp suddenly or quickly

   _____

2. **mean:** not nice; unkind

   _____

3. **smack:** to hit

   _____

4. **selfish:** wanting things only for yourself

   _____

5. **mock:** to make fun of

   _____

Score _____
(Top Score 5)

Teacher Read each word aloud. Have students write the vocabulary word from the box that means the same as the word that is shown.

Vocabulary List	3. wicked	7. mean
1. blame	4. cheat	8. nasty
2. slap	5. grab	9. pest
	6. greedy	10. tease

"Bad Behavior" Vocabulary • Word Meanings

Reference Skills

Glossary Sentences

pest	blame	Wicked	cheat	mean

_____

- - - - - - - - - - - - - - - - -

1. We _____ our dog for the muddy floor.

_____

- - - - - - - - - - - - - - - -

2. You are _____ to tease that dog.

_____

- - - - - - - - - - - - - -

3. We do not _____ when we play games.

_____

- - - - - - - - - - - - -

4. _____ people are not kind.

_____

- - - - - - - - - - - - -

5. A _____ is something that bothers you.

Teacher Read each incomplete sentence aloud to students. Have students use their glossary to look up each word in the word box. Then have students write the correct vocabulary word on the line in each sentence.

Score _____
(Top Score 5)

"Bad Behavior" Vocabulary • Reference Skills

③ Build New Vocabulary

Good and Bad

| cheat | wicked | helpful | kind | obey |
| cruel | gentle | greedy | nasty | share |

Good Behavior   Bad Behavior

_____   _____

- - - - - - - - - - - - - -   - - - - - - - - - - - - - -

_____   _____

- - - - - - - - - - - - - -   - - - - - - - - - - - - - -

_____   _____

- - - - - - - - - - - - - -   - - - - - - - - - - - - - -

_____   _____

- - - - - - - - - - - - - -   - - - - - - - - - - - - - -

_____   _____

- - - - - - - - - - - - - -   - - - - - - - - - - - - - -

_____   _____

Score _____
(Top Score 10)

Teacher Read each word aloud. Have students write each word from the box in the *Good Behavior* or the *Bad Behavior* category.

Vocabulary List	3. wicked	7. mean
1. blame	4. cheat	8. nasty
2. slap	5. grab	9. pest
	6. greedy	10. tease

"Bad Behavior" Vocabulary • Build New Vocabulary

 **Word Play**

Rhyming Clues

| blame | cheat | greedy | pest | slap |

1. _____   to <u>beat</u> by not playing fair

2. _____   to hit with a sound like a <u>clap</u>

3. _____   an unwanted <u>guest</u>

4. _____   to <u>shame</u>

5. _____   <u>needy</u> in a selfish way

Teacher Read each rhyming clue aloud. Have students write the word from the box that matches the definition and rhymes with the underlined word.

Score _____
(Top Score 5)

Vocabulary Review

1 **Review Word Meanings**

1. There were no people on the small <u>island</u>.

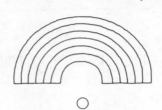      

2. The winds from the <u>hurricane</u> knocked over the tree.

3. The basement is a safe place to go during a <u>tornado</u>.

4. The weatherman said there would be heavy <u>snowfall</u>.

5. The sun set behind the <u>mountain</u>.

Score _____
(Top Score 5)

Teacher Read aloud the story on page 94 in the *Teacher's Edition* OR read the numbered sentences. Tell students to fill in the bubble below the picture that best matches the underlined word.

Vocabulary Review

② Review Word Meanings

1. The river flowed right through the <u>valley</u>.

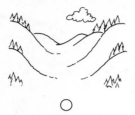 ○    ○    ○

2. The tractor pulled the <u>plow</u> over the field.

 ○    ○    ○

3. Rosa planted her <u>seed</u> in the garden.

 ○    ○    ○

4. Raymond used a <u>shovel</u> to dig a large hole.

 ○   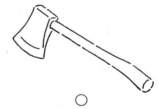 ○    ○

5. Then he used the <u>wheelbarrow</u> to haul away the dirt.

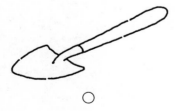 ○    ○    ○

Teacher Read aloud the story on page 95 in the *Teacher's Edition* OR read the numbered sentences. Tell students to fill in the bubble below the picture that best matches the underlined word.

Score _____
(Top Score 5)

③ Review Word Meanings

1. The fox ran into the <u>forest</u>.

   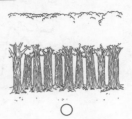   

   ○   ○   ○

2. The flower petals were wet from the morning <u>dew</u>.

   ○   ○   ○

3. Frogs were jumping in the <u>puddle</u>.

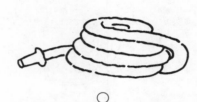      

   ○   ○   ○

4. She used the raft to <u>float</u> in the pool.

   ○   ○   ○

5. The mountain goat stood at the edge of the <u>cliff</u>.

      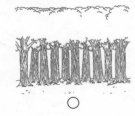

   ○   ○   ○

Score _____
(Top Score 5)

Teacher Read aloud the story on page 96 in the *Teacher's Edition* OR read the numbered sentences. Tell students to fill in the bubble below the picture that best matches the underlined word.

Review Word Meanings

1. The <u>greedy</u> man kept all the candy to himself.
   ○ nice   ○ angry   ○ selfish

2. We are not allowed to <u>slap</u> anyone at school.
   ○ smack   ○ silly   ○ pest

3. She said she would <u>grab</u> the toy from me if I did not give it to her.
   ○ blame   ○ snatch   ○ mean

4. Brian's mom told him not to <u>tease</u> his little sister.
   ○ slap   ○ plow   ○ mock

5. Everyone thought that the bully was <u>mean</u>.
   ○ unkind   ○ nice   ○ greedy

Teacher Read aloud the story on page 97 in the *Teacher's Edition* OR read the numbered sentences. Tell students to fill in the bubble next to the word that means the same as the underlined word.

Score _____
(Top Score 5)

"Journeys" Vocabulary

1   Word Meanings

Definitions

arrive	baggage	mile	prepare	travel

1. to get ready

   _____

2. to go on a trip

   _____

3. to get to a place

   _____

4. a unit of length that equals 5,280 feet

   _____

5. bags to carry things in

   _____

Score _____
(Top Score 5)

Teacher Read each word aloud. Have students write the vocabulary word from the box that matches the definition.

Vocabulary List	3. baggage	7. mile
1. rough	4. travel	8. passenger
2. arrive	5. tour	9. prepare
	6. sink	10. rest

"Journeys" Vocabulary • Word Meanings

Reference Skills

More Than One Meaning

1. sink

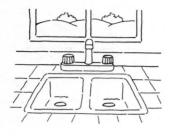 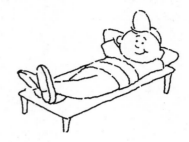

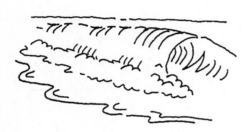 

rest	sink	tour

2. Mom says to put the dirty dishes in the

_____

_____ .

_____

3. After taking a _____ of the ship, the

_____

passengers wanted to sit down and _____ .

Teacher For the top part read the word *sink* aloud. Then have students circle the pictures that represent the two different meanings of *sink*. For the bottom part have students write the correct word from the word box in the blank. Each word is used once.

Score _____
(Top Score 5)

Irregular Past Tense

fell	flew	ran	threw	wrote

1. throw

_____
- - - - - - - - - - - - -
_____

2. write

_____
- - - - - - - - - - - - -
_____

3. run

_____
- - - - - - - - - - - - -
_____

4. fall

_____
- - - - - - - - - - - - -
_____

5. fly

_____
- - - - - - - - - - - - -
_____

Score _____
(Top Score 5)

Teacher Read each word aloud. Tell students to choose the irregular past tense of the word from the words in the box. Have them write the word they chose next to the matching picture.

Vocabulary	3. baggage	7. mile
List	4. travel	8. passenger
1. rough	5. tour	9. prepare
2. arrive	6. sink	10. rest

"Journeys" Vocabulary • Build New Vocabulary

Word Play

Changing Letters

c	g	k	p	w

1. <u>r</u>ough

2. mil<u>e</u>

3. <u>s</u>ink

4. sin<u>k</u>

5. <u>t</u>our

Teacher Read each word aloud. Have students identify the underlined letter in each word. Have students create new words by replacing the underlined letter with a letter from the box. Have them write the new word that matches the picture in the blank.

Score _____
(Top Score 5)

"Journeys" Vocabulary • Word Play

"Keep Trying" Vocabulary

1   Word Meanings

Synonyms

1. back   forward   advance

2. gift   game   contest

3. effort   stop   try

4. gain   win   lose

5. glory   honor   repeat

6. adjust   change   begin

Score _____
(Top Score 6)

Teacher Read each set of words aloud. Have students draw an X over the word that does not mean the same as the other two words.

Vocabulary List	3. advance	7. contest
1. adjust	4. gain	8. effort
2. champion	5. glory	9. almost
	6. repeat	10. finally

Reference Skills

Which Comes First?

1. almost   advance

_____
- - - - - - - - - - - - - -
_____

2. champion   contest

_____
- - - - - - - - - - - - - -
_____

3. glory   gain

_____
- - - - - - - - - - - - - -
_____

4. finally   forest

_____
- - - - - - - - - - - - - -
_____

5. effort   engine

_____
- - - - - - - - - - - - - -
_____

Teacher Read each pair of words aloud. Have students underline the second letter in each word. Then have them write the word that would come first alphabetically in the blank.

Score _____
(Top Score 15)

③ Build New Vocabulary

The Prefix *re-*

rebuild	refill	rewrite	reread	repaint

1.

_____

- - - - - - - - - - - - - - -

_____

2.

_____

- - - - - - - - - - - - - - -

_____

3.

_____

- - - - - - - - - - - - - - -

_____

4.

_____

- - - - - - - - - - - - - - -

_____

5.

_____

- - - - - - - - - - - - - - -

_____

Score _____
(Top Score 5)

Teacher Read each word in the box aloud. Have students write each word next to its matching picture.

Vocabulary List		
1. adjust	3. advance	7. contest
2. champion	4. gain	8. effort
	5. glory	9. almost
	6. repeat	10. finally

"Keep Trying" Vocabulary • Build New Vocabulary

Word Play

How Many Words?

champion

_____

- - - - - - - - - - - - - - - - - - -

_____

- - - - - - - - - - - - - - - - - - -

_____

- - - - - - - - - - - - - - - - - - -

_____

- - - - - - - - - - - - - - - - - - -

_____

- - - - - - - - - - - - - - - - - - -

_____

Teacher Have students create five new words
from the letters of the word _champion_ and write
them in the blanks.

Score _____
(Top Score 5)

"Shapes and Sizes" Vocabulary

1   **Word Meanings**

Picture Definitions

| curve | giant | heavy | straight | tiny |

1. _____

2. _____

3. _____

4. _____

5. _____

Teacher Read the words in the box aloud. Have students write each word next to its matching picture.

Vocabulary List	3. wide	7. thin
1. bent	4. spiral	8. curve
2. giant	5. heavy	9. tiny
	6. straight	10. flat

Reference Skills

Using a Glossary

bent	flat	giant	spiral	wide

1. The _____ mountain was very tall.

2. He gently _____ the tree branch.

3. The _____ stairs curved around to the second floor.

4. No one could jump across the _____ river.

5. A piece of paper is very _____ .

Teacher Read the words in the box aloud. Tell students to use their *Student Edition* glossary to look up each word. Have them write the missing word next to its correct sentence.

Score _____
(Top Score 5)

3 Build New Vocabulary

Antonyms

narrow	straight	light	big	thick

1. thin

2. tiny

3. wide

4. bent

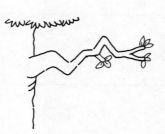

5. heavy

Score _____
(Top Score 5)

Teacher Read each word in the box aloud. Have students write each word next to the word and picture that have the opposite meaning.

Vocabulary List	3. wide	7. thin
	4. spiral	8. curve
1. bent	5. heavy	9. tiny
2. giant	6. straight	10. flat

"Shapes and Sizes" Vocabulary • Build New Vocabulary

 **Word Play**

Similes

| flat | heavy | tiny | wide |

1. I was so tired that my eyelids seemed as

   _____

   -

   _____ as a rock.

2. My baseball cap was as

   _____

   -

   _____ as a pancake

   after the car rolled over it.

3. Your smile is as _____

   as the ocean.

4. My little brother looked as

   _____

   -

   _____ as an ant next

   to the tall basketball player.

Teacher Read each word aloud. Have students
complete each simile by writing a word from the box
in the blank. Tell them to use the pictures for help.

Score _____
(Top Score 4)

Going to the Doctor's Office

1   **Word Meanings**

How Do You Feel?

accident	fever	heal	medicine	scratch

1.

2.

3.

4.

5.

Score _____
(Top Score 5)

Teacher Read the words in the box aloud. Have students write each word next to its matching picture.

Vocabulary List	3. ache	7. medicine
1. accident	4. fever	8. harm
2. heal	5. scratch	9. shiver
	6. pain	10. pale

Reference Skills

Which Is Correct?

1. aksident   accident   accedent

2. ache   ake   ach

3. feever   fevere   fever

4. haerm   harm   harme

5. shiver   chiver   shever

Teacher Read each word aloud. Have students draw a circle around the correct spelling of the word. They may use their glossaries for help.

Score _____
(Top Score 5)

3 Build New Vocabulary

Context Clues: Homophones

heal	heel	pail	pale

1. He could not get the sock over his

   _____

   – – – – – – – – – –

   _____.

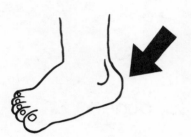

2. She carried the water home in a

   _____

   – – – – – – – – – –

   _____.

3. After seeing the scary movie, his face

   _____

   – – – – – – – – – –

   turned _____.

4. The doctor said that rest would help

   _____

   – – – – – – – – – –

   _____ her broken leg.

Score _____
(Top Score 4)

Teacher Read each word in the box and each sentence aloud. Have students complete each sentence with the correct word from the box.

Vocabulary List		
1. accident	3. ache	7. medicine
2. heal	4. fever	8. harm
	5. scratch	9. shiver
	6. pain	10. pale

Going to the Doctor's Office • Build New Vocabulary

Word Play

Scrambled Words

1. mahr

_____

- - - - - - - - - - - - - - -

_____

to cause pain

2. elap

_____

- - - - - - - - - - - - - - -

_____

having a white color; lacking color

3. verhis

_____

- - - - - - - - - - - - - - -

_____

to shake

4. chea

_____

- - - - - - - - - - - - - - -

_____

to be in constant pain

5. leha

_____

- - - - - - - - - - - - - - -

_____

to get well

6. inpa

_____

- - - - - - - - - - - - - - -

_____

a feeling of hurt

Teacher Tell students to unscramble each set of letters to form a vocabulary word. Have them write the word in the blank. Encourage them to use the definition hints for help.

Score _____
(Top Score 6)

Prepositions

1   **Word Meanings**

Examples

above	outside	through	on

_____

- - - - - - - - - - - -

1. The bird is _____

   its cage.

_____

- - - - - - - - - - - -

2. It flew _____

   the window.

3. Then the bird landed

   _____

   - - - - - - - - - - - -

   _____ the roof.

   _____

   - - - - - - - - - - - -

4. It flew high _____

   the house.

Teacher Read the words in the box and the sentences aloud. Tell students to look at each picture. Have them complete each sentence using a word from the box.

Vocabulary List	3. inside	7. below
	4. without	8. among
1. on	5. outside	9. beyond
2. along	6. above	10. through

Alphabetize By Second Letter

around	among	above	across	along

	Letter	Word
1.	_____	_____
2.	_____	_____
3.	_____	_____
4.	_____	_____
5.	_____	_____

Teacher Read each word from the box aloud. Have students write the second letter of each word in alphabetical order in the blanks under the *Letter* column. Then have them write the word that goes with each letter in the *Word* column.

Score _____
(Top Score 10)

Prepositions • Reference Skills

3 Build New Vocabulary

Up and *Out*

outfield	outfit	outgrow	uphill	upstairs

1. He put on his mitt as he ran into the

   _____

   - - - - - - - - - - - - - -

   _____ to play baseball.

   _____

   - - - - - - - - - - - - - -

2. All the bedrooms were _____ .

   _____

   - - - - - - - - - - - - - -

3. It is hard to pedal a bike _____ .

   _____

   - - - - - - - - - - - - - -

4. She decided to wear the red _____ .

   _____

   - - - - - - - - - - - - - -

5. Soon the baby will _____ these tiny

   clothes.

Score _____
(Top Score 5)

Teacher Read the words from the box and the sentences aloud. Have students complete each sentence with the correct compound word from the box.

Vocabulary List	3. inside	7. below
1. on	4. without	8. among
2. along	5. outside	9. beyond
	6. above	10. through

Prepositions • Build New Vocabulary

 **Word Play**

A or Be?

a	be

_____

1. under   _____low

2. over   _____bove

3. over the length of _____long

4. gone   _____way

5. at an earlier time _____fore

Teacher Read each short definition aloud. Have students complete the word that matches the definition by writing *a* or *be* in the blank.

Score _____
(Top Score 5)

Vocabulary Review

1   **Review Word Meanings**

1. Carlos liked to <u>travel</u> by bicycle.
   - ○ to fall to the bottom
   - ○ to take a trip
   - ○ to get ready

2. Alicia chose some books to <u>prepare</u> for the long bus ride.
   - ○ to take a trip
   - ○ to get ready
   - ○ to get to a place

3. Raul liked being a <u>passenger</u> on the boat.
   - ○ moving water
   - ○ a person who rides in a boat, airplane, or car
   - ○ suitcases and bags

4. The plane had to go to Chicago before it could <u>arrive</u> in New York.
   - ○ to get ready
   - ○ to take a trip
   - ○ to get to a place

5. Thankfully it would not be a <u>rough</u> trip.
   - ○ easy
   - ○ sandpaper
   - ○ difficult

Score _____
(Top Score 5)

Teacher Read aloud the story on page 118 in the *Teacher's Edition* OR read the numbered sentences. Tell students to fill in the bubble next to the definition that matches the underlined word.

Review Word Meanings

1. Eli was excited to win the <u>contest</u>.
   - ○ a game
   - ○ a try
   - ○ a winner

2. Marta had to <u>adjust</u> her glasses so she could see better.
   - ○ to do again
   - ○ to try
   - ○ to rearrange

3. It took a lot of <u>effort</u>, but we finally won the game.
   - ○ a game
   - ○ a winner
   - ○ a try

4. My little sister likes to <u>repeat</u> everything I say.
   - ○ to go forward
   - ○ to do again
   - ○ to win

5. Vince was considered to be a <u>champion</u> on the soccer field.
   - ○ a game
   - ○ a try
   - ○ a winner

Teacher Read aloud the story on page 119 in the *Teacher's Edition* OR read the numbered sentences. Tell students to fill in the bubble next to the definition that matches the underlined word.

Score _____
(Top Score 5)

③ Review Word Meanings

1. The rock was too <u>heavy</u> to move.

   ○      ○      ○

2. The path went <u>straight</u> into the forest.

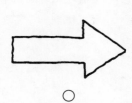   ○   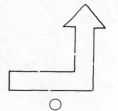   ○      ○

3. The bird was flying <u>through</u> the trees.

   ○      ○      ○

4. The bus slowed down as it went around the <u>curve</u>.

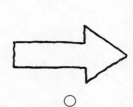   ○   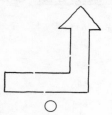   ○      ○

5. The bird flew high <u>above</u> the houses.

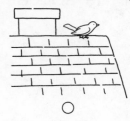   ○      ○      ○

Score _____
(Top Score 5)

Teacher Read aloud the story on page 120 in the *Teacher's Edition* OR read the numbered sentences. Tell students to fill in the bubble below the picture that best matches the underlined word.

 **Review Word Meanings**

1. The antenna on the television was <u>bent</u>.
   - ○ straight
   - ○ crooked
   - ○ flat

2. The cold wind made me <u>shiver</u>.
   - ○ shake
   - ○ ache
   - ○ pale

3. Pablo found a <u>scratch</u> on his knee.
   - ○ fever
   - ○ heal
   - ○ scrape

4. The water was <u>below</u> the bridge.
   - ○ under
   - ○ along
   - ○ beyond

5. Aunt Karen would not <u>harm</u> even a fly.
   - ○ heal
   - ○ hurt
   - ○ shiver

Teacher Read aloud the story on page 121 in the *Teacher's Edition* OR read the numbered sentences. Tell students to fill in the bubble next to the word that means the same as the underlined word.

Score _____
(Top Score 5)

"Being Afraid" Vocabulary

1 Word Meanings

Examples

1. hide

 ○

 ○

2. alley

 ○

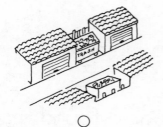 ○

3. blanket

 ○

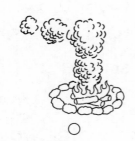 ○

4. howl

 ○

 ○

5. smoke

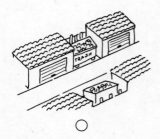 ○

 ○

Score _____
(Top Score 5)

Teacher Read each word aloud. Have students fill in the bubble below the picture that best matches the word.

Vocabulary List		
1. howl	3. alarm	7. smoke
2. blanket	4. hide	8. nothing
	5. nightmare	9. alley
	6. monster	10. cover

Reference Skills

Dictionary Definitions

alarm	monster	nightmare	nothing	cover

1. a scary, made-up creature

_____

2. a warning of danger

_____

3. not any thing

_____

4. a bad dream

_____

5. to be over the surface of; to hide from view

_____

Score _____
(Top Score 5)

3 Build New Vocabulary

Compound Words

bowling alley	hideout	smoke alarm
alarm clock	smokestack	

1. _____

2. _____

3. _____

4. _____

5. _____

Teacher Read each word aloud. Have students write each word from the box next to its matching picture.

Vocabulary List	3. alarm	7. smoke
	4. hide	8. nothing
1. howl	5. nightmare	9. alley
2. blanket	6. monster	10. cover

"Being Afraid" Vocabulary • Build New Vocabulary

 **Word Play**

Silly Rhymes

alley	howl	hide	nightmare	smoke

1. <u>Sally</u> kept a <u>tally</u> for the ant race in the

   _____

   - - - - - - - - - - -

   _____ .

                              _____

                              - - - - - - - - - - -

2. Did you see the elephants _____

   <u>inside</u> from the mouse they <u>spied</u>?

3. The <u>bear</u> and <u>Claire</u> had the same

   _____

   - - - - - - - - - - -

   _____ .

4. An <u>owl</u> on the <u>prowl</u> doesn't <u>growl</u> or

   _____

   - - - - - - - - - - -

   _____ .

                          _____

                          - - - - - - - - - - -

5. I <u>awoke</u> to _____

   coming from the <u>artichoke</u>.

Teacher Read each silly rhyme aloud. Have
students write the word from the box that best
completes each rhyme. (**HINT:** The word will rhyme
with the underlined word.)

Score _____
(Top Score 5)

More Animals

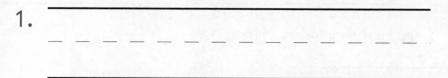

1   **Word Meanings**

Picture Definitions

1. _____

2. _____

3. _____

4. _____

5. _____

Score _____
(Top Score 5)

Teacher Have students write the correct animal name next to its picture.

Vocabulary List	3. caterpillar	7. butterfly
1. crab	4. beaver	8. turtle
2. chipmunk	5. dove	9. penguin
	6. ape	10. rabbit

Reference Skills

Guide Words

beaver	butterfly	caterpillar	penguin	rabbit

1. break/by

_____

- - - - - - - - - - - - - -

_____

2. pale/pot

_____

- - - - - - - - - - - - - -

_____

3. can/cave

_____

- - - - - - - - - - - - - -

_____

4. queen/rose

_____

- - - - - - - - - - - - - -

_____

5. back/box

_____

- - - - - - - - - - - - - -

_____

Teacher Read each pair of guide words aloud. Have students write each word from the box next to the guide words it can be found between.

Score _____
(Top Score 5)

Build New Vocabulary

Animal Characteristics

beaver	butterfly	crab	rabbit	turtle

1. long ears

_____

2. pretty wings

_____

3. pinching claws

_____

4. can hide its head
   inside its shell

_____

5. strong teeth for
   gnawing on wood

_____

Score _____
(Top Score 5)

Teacher Read each animal characteristic aloud. Have students write each word from the box next to the characteristic that describes that animal.

Vocabulary List	3. caterpillar	7. butterfly
	4. beaver	8. turtle
1. crab	5. dove	9. penguin
2. chipmunk	6. ape	10. rabbit

More Animals • Build New Vocabulary

Word Play

More Similes

| beaver | butterfly | rabbit | turtle |

1. Our old van moves as slowly as a

   _____

   _ _ _ _ _ _ _ _ _ _ _ _ _ _ _

   _____ .

   (has short legs and a curved shell)

2. Some goals are as hard to catch as a

   _____

   _ _ _ _ _ _ _ _ _ _ _ _ _ _ _

   _____ .

   (an insect)

3. My teacher says that I am as eager as a

   _____

   _ _ _ _ _ _ _ _ _ _ _ _ _ _ _

   _____ because I work so

   (its tail looks like a paddle)   hard in school.

4. When it comes to eating dessert, my sister is as quick as a

   _____

   _ _ _ _ _ _ _ _ _ _ _ _ _ _ _

   _____ .

   (some of these have cotton tails)

Teacher Read each incomplete simile aloud. Have students write the word from the box that best completes the simile. Encourage them to use the hints for help.

Score _____
(Top Score 4)

Parts of a House

Word Meanings

Describe It

ceiling	stairs	roof	chimney	dining room

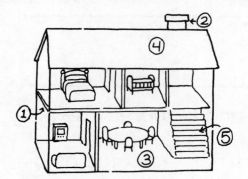

1. _____

2. _____

3. _____

4. _____

5. _____

Score _____
(Top Score 5)

Teacher Read the words from the box aloud. Have students write each word in the blank next to the correct location in the house.

Vocabulary List	3. dining room	7. garage
1. ceiling	4. nursery	8. cupboard
2. cellar	5. roof	9. porch
	6. chimney	10. stairs

 **Reference Skills**

Alphabetical Order

garage	dining room	porch	cupboard	nursery

1. couch

_____

- -

2. _____

3. desk

_____

- -

4. _____

5. fan

_____

- -

6. _____

7. house

_____

- -

8. _____

9. patio

_____

- -

10. _____

11. railing

Teacher Read each word aloud. Have students complete the list by writing the words from the box in alphabetical order.

Score _____
(Top Score 5)

Build New Vocabulary
Words That Go Together

cellar	chimney	cupboard	dining room	garage

1. basement

_____

- - - - - - - - - - - - - - - - - -

_____

2. shelf

_____

- - - - - - - - - - - - - - - - - -

_____

3. driveway

_____

- - - - - - - - - - - - - - - - - -

_____

4. table and chairs

_____

- - - - - - - - - - - - - - - - - -

_____

5. fireplace

_____

- - - - - - - - - - - - - - - - - -

_____

Score _____
(Top Score 5)

Teacher Read each word aloud. Have students write the word from the box next to its related word or words.

Vocabulary List		
1. ceiling	3. dining room	7. garage
2. cellar	4. nursery	8. cupboard
	5. roof	9. porch
	6. chimney	10. stairs

Parts of a House • Build New Vocabulary

Word Play

Things That Go Together

ceiling	dining room	garage	nursery	porch

1. _____

2. _____

3. _____

4. _____

5. _____

Teacher Read the words from the box aloud. Have students write each word next to the picture that it best relates to.

Score _____
(Top Score 5)

"Movement" Vocabulary

1   Word Meanings

Demonstrate

chase	grip	pass	throw	tumble

1. tip

2. race

3. jumble

4. go

5. grass

Teacher Read the words aloud.
Have students write each word
from the box next to its rhyming
word and matching picture.

Vocabulary List	3. dodge	7. grip
	4. drift	8. throw
1. dart	5. tumble	9. dash
2. pass	6. chase	10. roll

"Movement" Vocabulary • Word Meanings

Glossary Sentences

grip	dodge	pass	chase	drift

_____

- - - - - - - - - - - - - - -

1. You should _____ the football to

   another player.

_____

- - - - - - - - - - - - - - -

2. Try to _____ the ball and not get hit.

_____

- - - - - - - - - - - - - - -

3. Cats like to _____ mice.

_____

- - - - - - - - - - - - - - -

4. _____ the baseball bat with both hands.

_____

- - - - - - - - - - - - - - -

5. We let our boat _____ down the river.

Teacher Read each incomplete sentence aloud to students. Have them use their glossary to look up each word in the word box. Then have them write the correct vocabulary word on the line in each sentence.

Score _____
(Top Score 5)

"Movement" Vocabulary • Reference Skills

③ Build New Vocabulary

Context Clues

1. After he hit the ball with the club, we watched it <u>roll</u> into the hole.

 ○    ○    ○

2. Marc <u>dashed</u> across the ice to get to the puck.

 ○   ○    ○

3. The coach told me to <u>grip</u> the football tightly.

 ○   ○   ○

4. Anita wanted to <u>tumble</u> three times over the mat before doing a cartwheel.

 ○    ○   ○

5. The goalie <u>dodged</u> the ball at first, but Tammy still kicked it in to score a goal.

 ○   ○   ○

Score _____
(Top Score 5)

Teacher Read each sentence aloud. Have students fill in the bubble below the picture of the sport or game that the sentence describes.

Vocabulary List	3. dodge	7. grip
1. dart	4. drift	8. throw
2. pass	5. tumble	9. dash
	6. chase	10. roll

"Movement" Vocabulary • Build New Vocabulary

Word Play

Crossword Puzzle

| carriage | cupboard | dodge | fog | pass |
| coop | dart | drift | grip | roll |

Across

2. a place for dishes
5. turn over and over
6. thick mist
8. move quickly and suddenly
9. jump aside

Down

1. a cart drawn by horses
2. home for a chicken
3. throw
4. float
7. hold tightly

Teacher Have students read each clue and then complete the crossword puzzle using the words from the box.

Score _____
(Top Score 10)

Useful Objects

1   **Word Meanings**

Examples

basket	hook	knob	pot	toothbrush

1.

_____

- - - - - - - - - - - - - - - - -

_____

2.

_____

- - - - - - - - - - - - - - - - -

_____

3.

_____

- - - - - - - - - - - - - - - - -

_____

4.

_____

- - - - - - - - - - - - - - - - -

_____

5.

_____

- - - - - - - - - - - - - - - - -

_____

Score _____
(Top Score 5)

Teacher Read the words in the box aloud. Have students write each word next to its matching picture.

Vocabulary List	3. rope	7. rag
1. hook	4. thimble	8. bowl
2. knob	5. toothbrush	9. basket
	6. pot	10. dish

Useful Objects • Word Meanings

Reference Skills

Dictionary Sentences

1. We eat soup from a <u>bowl</u>.

A.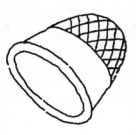

2. A <u>rag</u> is used for cleaning.

B.

3. She wears a <u>thimble</u> while she sews.

C.

4. We used the <u>rope</u> to pull the boat to shore.

D.

5. Mom put the chicken on the <u>dish</u>.

E.

Teacher Read each sentence aloud. Have students draw a line from the sentence to its matching picture.

Score _____
(Top Score 5)

Build New Vocabulary

Useful Uses

dish	hook	pot	rag	thimble

1. cleaning _____

2. eating _____

3. sewing _____

4. cooking _____

5. hanging _____

Score _____
(Top Score 5)

Teacher Read each word aloud. Have students write the word from the box next to the word that best describes its use.

Vocabulary List	3. rope	7. rag
	4. thimble	8. bowl
1. hook	5. toothbrush	9. basket
2. knob	6. pot	10. dish

Useful Objects • Build New Vocabulary

Word Play

Rhymes

bowl	dish	hook	pot	rope

1. a <u>fish</u> on a _____

2. <u>soap</u> on a _____

3. a very <u>hot</u> _____

4. a <u>hole</u> in a _____

5. a _____ over a <u>brook</u>

Teacher Read each incomplete rhyme aloud. Have students write the word from the box that best completes the rhyme. (**Hint:** The underlined words rhyme with the correct word.)

Score _____
(Top Score 5)

Vocabulary Review

1   Review Word Meanings

1. We watched the <u>penguin</u> dive into the water.

   ○   ○   ○

2. Even though the fire was out, he could still see <u>smoke</u>.

      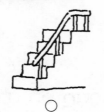

   ○   ○   ○

3. The baby slept quietly in the <u>nursery</u>.

   ○   ○   ○

4. The <u>ape</u> climbed the tree to reach the fruit.

   ○   ○   ○

5. Aunt Mae carried the eggs in her <u>basket</u>.

   ○   ○   ○

Score _____
(Top Score 5)

Teacher Read aloud the story on page 142 in the *Teacher's Edition* OR read the numbered sentences. Tell students to fill in the bubble below the picture that best matches the underlined word.

② Review Word Meanings

1. Grandma likes to eat dinner in the <u>dining room</u>.

○   ○   ○

2. Juan stacked the plates in the <u>cupboard</u>.

  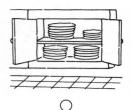

○   ○   ○

3. Aunt Maria planted a seed in the <u>pot</u>.

○   ○   ○

4. A <u>thimble</u> protects your finger when you sew.

  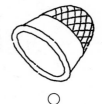

○   ○   ○

5. The <u>caterpillar</u> made its chrysalis under the leaf.

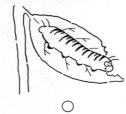  

○   ○   ○

Teacher Read aloud the story on page 143 in the *Teacher's Edition* OR read the numbered sentences. Tell students to fill in the bubble below the picture that best matches the underlined word.

Score _____
(Top Score 5)

Vocabulary Review

Review Word Meanings

1. Luisa turned the <u>knob</u> to open the door.

   ◯      ◯   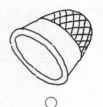   ◯

2. We watched the toy sailboat <u>drift</u> down the river.

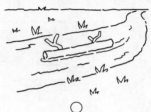   ◯      ◯      ◯

3. Uncle Phil parked his car in the <u>garage</u>.

   ◯      ◯      ◯

4. I hung my coat on the <u>hook</u>.

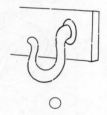   ◯      ◯      ◯

5. Mom lets us <u>throw</u> pennies into the fountain.

   ◯      ◯   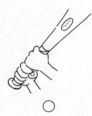   ◯

Score _____
(Top Score 5)

Teacher Read aloud the story on page 144 in the *Teacher's Edition* OR read the numbered sentences. Tell students to fill in the bubble below the picture that best matches the underlined word.

Vocabulary Review

 **Review Word Meanings**

1. Mother stored the old toys in the <u>cellar</u>.

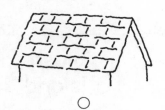      

◯   ◯   ◯

2. We had to <u>grip</u> the rope to pull the boat to shore.

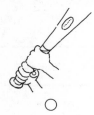      

◯   ◯   ◯

3. The <u>crab</u> walked across the sand.

      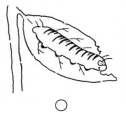

◯   ◯   ◯

4. Pedro used the <u>rope</u> to tie the stacks of newspaper.

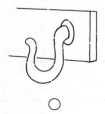      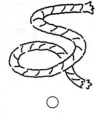

◯   ◯   ◯

5. The cat would <u>hide</u> whenever the dog came into the room.

◯   ◯   ◯

Teacher Read aloud the story on page 145 in the *Teacher's Edition* OR read the numbered sentences. Tell students to fill in the bubble below the picture that best matches the underlined word.

Score _____
(Top Score 5)

Cumulative Review

Definitions

| backpack | nursery | sink | blush |
| howl | music | finish | island |

1. You can carry your books in it

   _____

2. A small piece of land surrounded by water

   _____

3. A room for a baby

   _____

4. You can listen to this on the radio

   _____

5. A loud sound a wolf makes

   _____

6. If a boat has a leak, it will do this

   _____

Score _____
(Top Score 6)

Teacher Tell students to read each clue carefully. Then have them select the word from the box that best fits the clue and write it in the blank. Two words will not be used.

Synonyms

1.    morning   night   dawn

2.    kick   throw   toss

3.    pile   heap   exact

4.    cottage   park   cabin

5.    tiny   giant   big

6.    ready   end   finish

Teacher Tell students to look carefully at each picture as you read each word choice aloud. Have them draw an X over the word that does NOT represent the picture.

Score _____
(Top Score 6)

Sentence Completion

Quack	Polite	crab	cow
plumber	crowd	giggle	

_____

1. _____ people say "Please" and

"Thank you."

_____

2. The _____ came to fix the

water pipes.

_____

3. We saw a _____ walking on

the beach.

_____

4. There was a big _____ of people

at the circus.

_____

5. I heard the duck say, "_____."

Score _____
(Top Score 5)

Teacher Read each incomplete sentence aloud.
Have students select the word from the box
that best completes each sentence and write
it in the blank. Two words will not be used.

Words and Themes

1.  factory   Useful Objects

2. 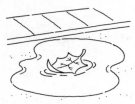 puddle   Movement

3.  bicycle   Things That Go

4.  rope   Water

5.  grandmother   Family

6.  tumble   Our Neighborhood at Work

Teacher Read each word and theme aloud. Tell students to draw a line from the word on the left to the correct theme on the right. Have them complete this exercise without looking back at the Vocabulary Lists in each lesson.

Score _____
(Top Score 6)

Word Webs

You can draw a word web. A **word web** helps you think of words that are related.

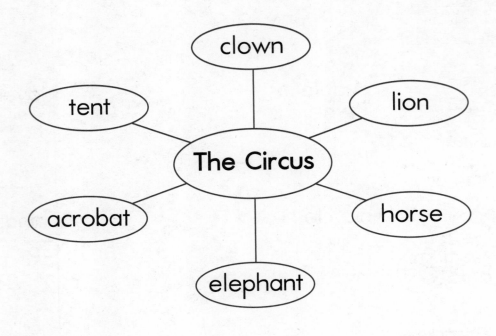

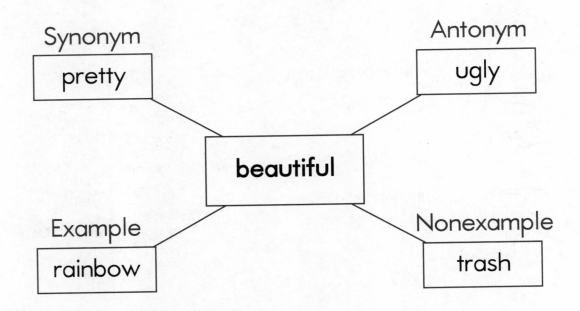

Categorization

You can place words into categories, or groups.

Words That Begin With "b"

basket	begin
bowl	below
bent	behave

The words in each category have something in common.

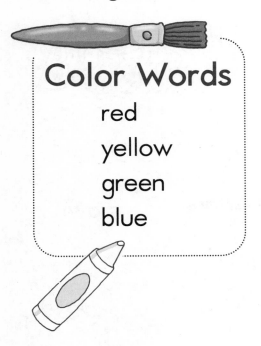

Color Words

red
yellow
green
blue

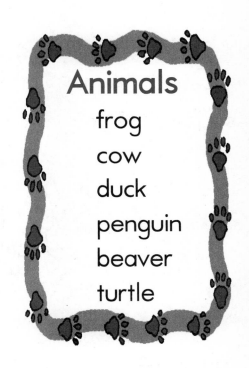

Animals
frog
cow
duck
penguin
beaver
turtle

Weather Words

rain	frost
snow	cloud
sunshine	thunder

Linear Graphs

A **linear graph** is another way to show how words are related.

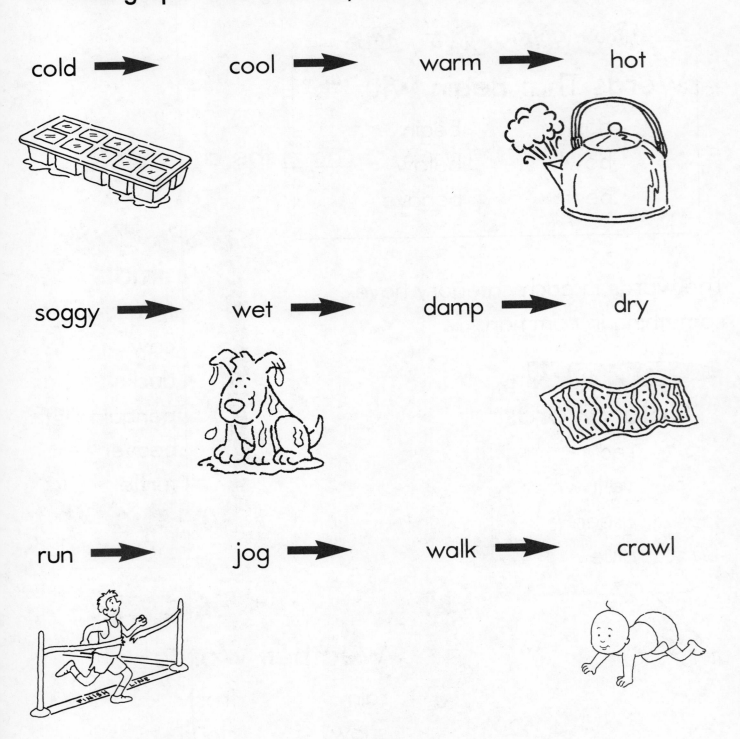

cold ➡ cool ➡ warm ➡ hot

soggy ➡ wet ➡ damp ➡ dry

run ➡ jog ➡ walk ➡ crawl

Cool is warmer than **cold**. **Warm** is cooler than **hot**.

Context Clues

A **context clue** is a clue to the meaning of a word.

New Word

The dog likes to <u>chase</u> the cat.

Context Clue

Chase means "to run after something."

. . . .

New Word

The <u>tale</u>, "Jack and the Beanstalk," is a fun story to read.

Context Clue

Tale means "story."

Context Clues

You can use context clues when you read. They help you learn more words.

The bus ride to the museum was long, but our visit was **brief.** We stayed at the museum for only one hour.

Can you see clues in the sentences that tell what *brief* means?

How to Use Context Clues

1. Look at the sentence.
2. Point to the word or words you do not know.
3. Ask yourself, "Is the meaning of the word in the sentence?"
4. Ask yourself, "Is the opposite meaning of the word in the sentence?"
5. Look at the sentences before and after to find more clues.

Word Relationships

Antonyms have opposite meanings.

Antonyms

new/old   above/below

cool/warm   open/close

short/tall   push/pull

up/down   happy/sad

··

Synonyms have the same or about the same meanings.

Synonyms

begin/start   crooked/bent

mad/angry   fast/quick

close/shut   old/ancient

end/finish   yell/shout

Word Relationships

Word Families

The words in a **word family** have some of the same sounds and letters in them.

The *it* Word Family

it	bit	sit
kit	pit	wit
hit	fit	

The *all* Word Family

ball	stall	tall
call	small	wall
fall	hall	

Homophones and Homographs

Homophones are words that sound the same but are not spelled the same. They have different meanings.

Homophones

hare/hair	new/knew	sun/son
bare/bear	see/sea	two/to

Homographs are words that look the same but have different meanings.

Homographs

bat: a flying animal	wind: the air that blows
bat: a club for hitting a	outside
baseball	wind: to turn many times

Building Vocabulary Skills
Level 1
Home Connection

To Reinforce Vocabulary Skills at Home

Tools and Reference

Table of Contents

Words in Another Country . . . . .T&R2
Prefixes and Suffixes .T&R3
Base Words . . . . .T&R4
Italian Words . . . . .T&R5
Fun With Words . . . . .T&R6
Dictionary Skills . . . . .T&R7
Nouns, Verbs, and Adjectives . . . . .T&R9

Glossary . . . . .T&R10

Word Bank . . . . .T&R29

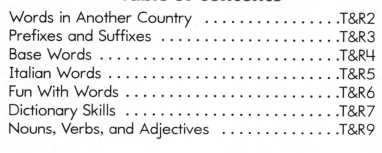

www.sra4kids.com

Send all inquiries to:
SRA/McGraw-Hill
8787 Orion Place
Columbus, OH 43240-4027

Printed in the United States of America.

R00004409

2 3 4 5 6 7 8 9 QPD 07 06 05 04 03

Columbus, OH • Chicago, IL • Redmond, WA

The McGraw-Hill Companies

Words in Another Country

Note to Home Use this page as a fun reference for pointing out the different words used for common objects in the United States and Great Britain. This will help your student begin to understand the cultural nature of words. You may wish to show your student where Great Britain is located on a map or globe.

Compare the American word to the British word for the same thing.

American Words	British Words
cracker	biscuit
apartment	flat
principal	headmaster or headmistress
stove	cooker
soccer	football
sidewalk	pavement or footpath
raincoat	mackintosh
trunk (of a car)	boot
elevator	lift
windshield	windscreen

Try putting the British word in place of the boldfaced American word in these sentences:

I like to eat **crackers** and jam.

Is there a **sidewalk** in front of your **apartment?**

The **principal**'s **raincoat** is bright green.

Prefixes and Suffixes

Note to Home Read this page with your student. Use it as a reference for identifying words that have prefixes and suffixes in books you read together.

Prefixes

A **prefix** can be at the beginning of a word.

Prefix	Meaning	Example Word
pre-	before	preview = to view before (a movie preview)
re-	again	rewrite = to write again
un-	not; opposite	unlock = opposite of lock unwanted = not wanted

The teacher told me to *rewrite* my messy paper.

Suffixes

A **suffix** can be at the end of a word.

Suffix	Meaning	Example Word
-er	one who	farmer = one who farms
-less	without	tasteless = without taste
-ful	full of	joyful = full of joy

The pretty music makes me feel *joyful.*

Base Words

Note to Home Read this page with your student. Help him or her identify the prefixes or suffixes in the second list below (*-er, -ing, un-, -s, re-, -ed, -ness, -ly*). Extend learning by helping your student identify base words in books you read together.

A **base word** is a word without a prefix or suffix.

Base Words		
sing	wash	shy
lock	finish	equal

Words With Prefixes or Suffixes			
singer	*unlock*	*rewash*	*shyness*
singing	*locks*	*finished*	*equally*

Italian Words

Note to Home Many common words in the English language are borrowed, or adapted, from a foreign language. Use this page as a fun reference to help your student learn some American words that are also Italian words. You may wish to show your student where Italy is located on a map or globe.

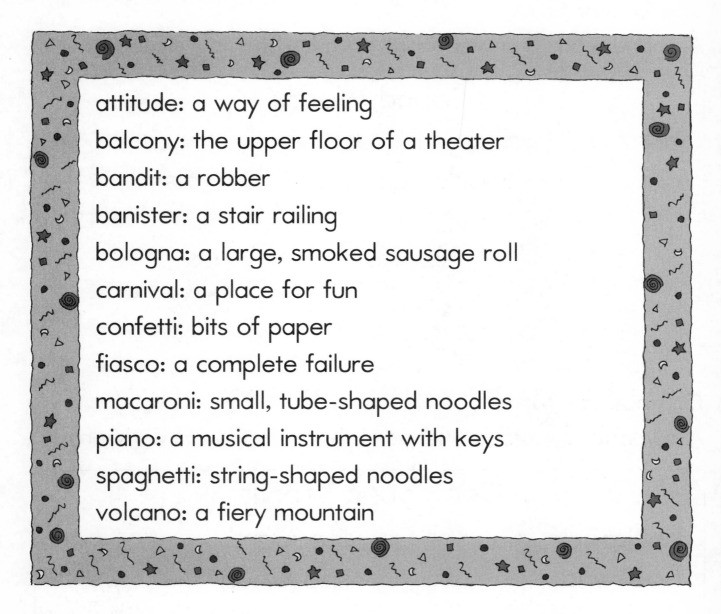

attitude: a way of feeling

balcony: the upper floor of a theater

bandit: a robber

banister: a stair railing

bologna: a large, smoked sausage roll

carnival: a place for fun

confetti: bits of paper

fiasco: a complete failure

macaroni: small, tube-shaped noodles

piano: a musical instrument with keys

spaghetti: string-shaped noodles

volcano: a fiery mountain

To keep from falling down the stairs, hold onto the **banister.**

We made **confetti** with colored tissue paper to throw during the parade.

Fun With Words

Note to Home Read this page with your student. Ask him or her to identify objects or animals that match each sound word. Then help your student identify the two words in each compound word.

Sound Words

A **sound word** is a word that sounds like what it means.

Sound Words			
buzz	ring	boom	roar
chirp	quack	moo	hiss

Compound Words

A **compound word** is one word that is made of two words.

Compound Words	
backpack	lifeguard
bookend	snowman
cupboard	seashell
skateboard	toothbrush

Dictionary Skills

Note to Home If you have a picture dictionary, refer to it as you read this page with your student. Help your student look up his or her favorite words.

A **dictionary** is a book that lists words and their meanings. Some dictionaries have pictures to show you what the words mean.

canoe

nursery

tornado

A dictionary may also show the word in a sentence.

The children paddled their **canoe** *down the stream.*

My baby sister was asleep in her crib in the **nursery.**

The safest place to be during a **tornado** *is in the basement.*

Dictionary Skills

Note to Home Read this page with your student. Quiz him or her on alphabetical order by using the vocabulary words in this book. For example, "Which word comes first in the dictionary—*grip* or *ache?*"

ABC Order

The words in a dictionary are in ABC order. This is also called alphabetical order.

> A B C D E F G H I J K L M N
> O P Q R S T U V W X Y Z
> a b c d e f g h i j k l m n
> o p q r s t u v w x y z

To find a word in a dictionary, you need to know its beginning letter.

Beginning Letter

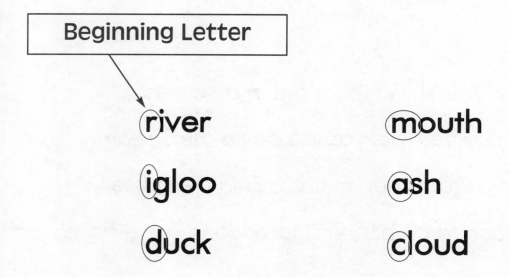

river   mouth

igloo   ash

duck   cloud

Nouns, Verbs, and Adjectives

Note to Home Read this page with your student to introduce parts of speech. Choose a book that contains simple sentences, and lead your student in identifying nouns, verbs, and adjectives.

Nouns

A **noun** names things, people, animals, or places.

Nouns			
bowl	lake	thimble	garage
nest	penguin	soil	fish

Verbs

A **verb** shows an action or tells what something or someone is or has.

Verbs			
roll	blink	pretend	fill
howl	obey	speak	drift

Adjectives

An **adjective** tells more about a noun.

Adjectives			
silly	heavy	polite	rough

We made **silly** faces to make our teacher laugh.

The table is too **heavy** to move by myself.

Note to Home The glossary provides a meaningful context for each vocabulary word presented in this book. Use it as a reference to reinforce your student's understanding of the vocabulary words.

Glossary

A a

about This book is **about** a green frog.

above We saw hundreds of stars in the sky **above** us.

accident It was an **accident** when I hurt my arm.

ache My fingers **ache** because I hurt them.

adjust **Adjust** your belt so it is not too tight.

advance I will **advance** one grade this year.

airplane People ride in an **airplane** high in the sky.

alarm We heard an **alarm** when we opened the fire exit door.

alley 1. We walked in the **alley** between the buildings. 2. We go to the bowling **alley** on Saturdays.

almost I **almost** dropped my cup, but I did not drop it.

along We walked **along** the country road.

already I was not hungry because I had **already** eaten.

always I **always** wash in the bathtub.

among They sit **among** other students at lunchtime.

angry The boy was **angry** when the toy broke.

ape An **ape** looks like a large monkey with no tail.

arrive My grandmother will **arrive** in Dallas at five o'clock today.

ash The wood in the fireplace burned to **ash.**

ax He used an **ax** to chop wood for our fire.

B b

backpack I carry books in my **backpack.**

baggage Take only two suitcases as **baggage.**

basket We carried our lunch in a picnic **basket.**

batch We baked a **batch** of muffins.

beautiful The cat had **beautiful,** shiny fur.

beaver A **beaver** has sharp front teeth and lives by streams.

bee A **bee** is an insect that makes honey.

begin To **begin** means to start.

behave My dogs **behave** at home and do not bite.

belong You **belong** to your family.

below We saw snow on the road **below** our window.

bent He gently **bent** the tree branch, but did not break it.

beyond Our house is **beyond** those trees.

bicycle I put air into both tires on my **bicycle.**

bird A **bird** has feathers and lays eggs.

blame We **blame** our dog for the muddy floor.

blanket She lies under a **blanket** to keep warm.

blessing The rain was a **blessing** for the flowers.

blink To **blink** means to quickly open and close your eyes.

blush My face turns red when I **blush.**

bookend A **bookend** holds books in line.

borrow You may **borrow** the book from the library, but you must return it in two weeks.

bowl I eat oatmeal from a blue **bowl.**

building My mother works in a tall **building.**

bunch That is a big **bunch** of purple grapes.

bundle I tied the **bundle** of papers with string.

bushel A **bushel** is a way to measure grain.

butterfly A **butterfly** has a thin body and four wings.

C c

cabin Abraham Lincoln lived in a log **cabin.**

cage My bird lives in a **cage.**

canoe We paddled our **canoe** down the river.

canyon A **canyon** is a deep valley with steep sides.

carriage The queen rode in a golden **carriage.**

cart A gray horse pulled the **cart.**

cat Our **cat** has whiskers and a long tail.

caterpillar A **caterpillar** looks like a short worm and turns into a butterfly.

cave The **cave** was a big hole in the rocks.

ceiling The **ceiling** of the room is above us.

cellar We store extra food and clothing down in our **cellar.**

champion Our winning team is the **champion.**

chase Our cat likes to **chase** mice in the field.

chatter The happy people **chatter** and talk.

cheat We do not **cheat** when playing games.

child The new baby is a young **child.**

chimney A **chimney** carries smoke away from a fireplace.

chipmunk A **chipmunk** has dark stripes on its back.

chirp   We heard the birds **chirp** outside.

circle   If I draw a ball, I draw a **circle.**

clerk   The **clerk** helped me find a new shirt.

cliff   We saw the valley from the top of a high **cliff.**

cloud   The **cloud** in the sky blocked the sun.

clown   A **clown** wears funny clothes and makes us laugh.

contest   My friend won the swimming **contest.**

coop   We keep our chickens in a **coop.**

cottage   We live in a **cottage** by the lake.

cousin   The child of your aunt or uncle is your **cousin.**

cover   A hat will **cover** your head.

cow   The **cow** was quiet when the farmer milked her.

crab   A **crab** has a hard shell and two claws.

croak   Big frogs sit and **croak** by the pond.

crowd   A large **crowd** of people waited to enter the circus tent.

cupboard   Our glasses and dishes are in this **cupboard.**

curve   A **curve** is a line that is not straight.

D d

daily **Daily** means every day.

dart We saw a rabbit **dart** into the bushes.

dash The dogs **dash** after the rabbit.

dawn The sun rises at **dawn.**

den The bear lay sleeping in his **den.**

depend My birds **depend** on me to feed them.

deserve You **deserve** praise for your good work.

dew The **dew** on the grass made my feet wet.

dining room We have dinner every night in the **dining room.**

dish I put my sandwich on a **dish.**

dodge Try to **dodge** the ball and not get hit.

dog My **dog** barks and has floppy ears.

double **Double** means two times as much.

dove The **dove** made a cooing sound.

dozen One **dozen** is a group of 12 things.

drift We let our boat **drift** down the river.

drowsy I feel **drowsy** when I lie in bed.

duck A **duck** is a bird who likes water.

due My book is **due** at the library today.

E e

east The sun rises in the **east.**

effort Climbing a mountain takes a lot of **effort.**

elephant The **elephant** picked up a peanut with its trunk.

enough We had **enough** players for a baseball game.

equal To be **equal** means to be the same.

exact The clock shows the **exact** time.

F f

factory This **factory** makes farm machinery.

fever He had a **fever** because his temperature was 102 degrees.

field The **field** was full of tall corn.

fill Please **fill** this glass with water.

finally We **finally** got home after the storm.

fine 1. I had to pay a **fine** at the library.
2. The weather is **fine** today.

finish Please **finish** your homework before dinner.

fish The **fish** swam in the fishbowl.

flat A piece of paper is very **flat.**

float I can **float** on my back in the pool.

fly **1.** A **fly** is a flying insect. **2.** I like to **fly** my kite in the park.

fog We could not see through the white **fog.**

folks A lot of **folks** waited in line for a ticket.

forest Many trees and plants live in the **forest.**

frog The green **frog** hops into the pond.

frost It is so cold that there is **frost** on our car.

frown Her **frown** showed she was sad.

G g

gain You can **gain** strength by lifting weights.

garage We keep our bikes and our car in the **garage.**

gentle The **gentle** horse was easy to ride.

giant **1.** The **giant** mountain was very tall.
2. The **giant** in the story was a tall person.

giggle My sisters **giggle** at my jokes.

glad I smile when I am **glad.**

glory He gained **glory** when he won the race.

grab Do not **grab** a bone from a dog.

grandfather My **grandfather** is my mother's father.

grandmother Our **grandmother** is our father's mother.

greedy **Greedy** people are often selfish.

greet I **greet** you by saying "Hi."

grin I have a **grin** on my face when I am happy.

grip **Grip** the baseball bat with both hands.

groan I **groan** when I bang my foot.

guess You should **guess** the answer to a joke.

H h

handmade My grandmother made me a **handmade** blanket.

handsome The **handsome** man had a nice smile.

harm It is mean to **harm** animals.

heal This bandage will help **heal** your cut.

heap A **heap** of hay lay by the barn.

heavy The chair is too **heavy** for you to lift.

hide I **hide** when I do not want someone to see me.

hole First we dig a **hole** for our seed, then we plant it.

honest I am **honest** and say what is true.

hook Please hang your coat on the coat **hook**.

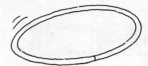

hoop The lion at the circus jumped through the **hoop.**

horse The cowgirl rode her **horse** in the rodeo.

hose We water our garden with a **hose.**

howl Wolves and dogs both **howl.**

hum You can **hum** a song with no words.

hurricane A **hurricane** is a storm that begins in the ocean.

hut Their **hut** had a roof made of hay.

I i

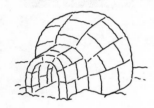

ice Water that is frozen is called **ice.**

igloo An **igloo** is a house made of ice and snow.

ink I write with the **ink** in my pen.

inside I put the food **inside** my mouth.

instant An **instant** is just a moment.

island An **island** is a piece of land with water all around it.

K k

knob A **knob** is a round handle.

L l

lake A **lake** is a body of water with land all around it.

leak The rain will **leak** through the hole in the roof.

lifeguard The **lifeguard** at the beach keeps swimmers safe.

lion The **lion** is a member of the cat family.

live Lots of animals **live** at the zoo.

lucky I was **lucky** to win a prize.

M m

mask Wearing a **mask** makes your face look different.

mean You are **mean** to tease that dog.

medicine **Medicine** can help a sick person feel better.

members My cousins and I are **members** of the same family.

mile If you walk a **mile,** you walk 5,280 feet.

minute One **minute** has sixty seconds.

monster The **monster** in my dream scared me.

motor The fan's **motor** makes it blow air.

mountain A **mountain** is much bigger than a hill.

mouth I hum with my **mouth** closed.

music We sing during **music** class.

N n

nasty Do not say **nasty** things about your little brother.

nature The forests and the mountains are part of **nature.**

nest There was a blue egg in the bird's **nest.**

nice The **nice** girl was kind to everyone.

nightmare A **nightmare** is just a bad dream.

north Canada is **north** of the United States.

nothing **Nothing** is scary to that brave girl.

nursery A **nursery** is a baby's bedroom.

O o

obey When I **obey,** I do what I am told.

ocean An **ocean** is made of salt water.

office She works in an **office.**

on Please put your books **on** the desk.

operator The **operator** of a bulldozer should wear a hard hat.

outside 1. I like to play in the park **outside**.
2. The **outside** of our house is blue.

overflow 1. Water in a bathtub can **overflow**.
2. We can mop the **overflow** on the floor.

P p

page I like the pictures on that **page** of the book.

pain I have a **pain** in my arm and it hurts.

pale Your face looks **pale** and you seem sick.

paper I drew a bird on my blue **paper**.

parent A father or a mother is a **parent**.

pass 1. You should **pass** the football to another player. 2. He threw a **pass** and won the football game.

passenger A **passenger** next to me on the bus was sleeping.

past Dinosaurs lived in the **past**.

penguin A **penguin** is a bird that swims but cannot fly.

pest A **pest** is something that bothers you.

plow 1. We watched the farmer **plow** his field.
2. The **plow** turned the dirt over.

plumber The **plumber** fixed the leaking pipe.

police The **police** help to keep us safe.

polite Be **polite** and say "Please."

porch There was a white swing on the front **porch.**

pot She cooked the soup in a big **pot.**

prairie A **prairie** is flat land covered with grass.

prepare We must **prepare** for our trip by packing our bags.

present 1. The **present** is now. 2. I open my birthday **present.**

pretend I like to **pretend** I can fly.

print The names on the map are in small **print.**

prize We won a **prize** at the school fair.

promise When I **promise** to clean my room, I do it.

puddle A small pool of water is a **puddle.**

Q q

quack The **quack** of a duck makes me giggle.

R r

rabbit A **rabbit** has long ears and soft fur.

rag Use this old **rag** to wipe the floor.

rain **Rain** falls from the clouds and waters the flowers.

rainbow We saw the colors of a **rainbow** in the sky.

ready We get **ready** to go to school in the morning.

related My cousin and I are **related** to each other.

repeat Would you please **repeat** your question?

rest 1. Remember to **rest** when you feel tired.
2. Did you get enough **rest** last night?

return Please **return** this book to the library today.

river We saw fish swimming in the **river.**

roar The **roar** of the lion was loud.

roll I trained the dog to **roll** over.

roof The **roof** of the cabin was made of tin.

rope 1. I like to jump with this **rope.**
2. The cowboy **roped** the cow.

rough A cat's tongue is **rough** like sandpaper.

S s

scooter A **scooter** has two wheels and a handle to hold on to.

scratch I had a **scratch** on my leg from the cat.

seed A nut is a **seed** from a tree.

sentence Write a **sentence** about your trip.

shiver The cold air made me **shiver.**

shovel **1.** Use a **shovel** to dig a big hole.
2. We **shovel** the dirt into the hole.

show **1.** The circus was a fun **show.**
2. You **show** your ticket at the gate.

shy My sister is **shy** and hides from visitors.

silly When I hear **silly** songs, I laugh.

singer My mother is a **singer** in the choir.

sink **1.** We watched the sun **sink** below the hills.
2. Please put your glass in the **sink.**

skateboard A **skateboard** is a flat board with four wheels that you ride standing up.

slap Do not **slap** anyone in the face.

smile **1.** A **smile** is a way to say "Hello."
2. Please **smile** for the camera.

smoke Only a cloud of **smoke** was left from the fire.

snowfall The **snowfall** today left heaps of snow.

soil The farmer planted seeds in the **soil.**

sometime She came here **sometime** last summer.

south Mexico is **south** of the United States.

speak To **speak** means to talk.

spiral The **spiral** stairs curved around to the second floor.

squeal I heard the pig **squeal** in the barnyard.

stairs **Stairs** are steps that you can go up or down.

story I wrote a **story** about tigers.

straight The highway had a **straight** line down the middle.

study My sister will **study** for her test.

suddenly **Suddenly** we heard thunder.

sunny The **sunny** sky had no clouds.

support My mother will **support** me and take care of me.

surprise A secret birthday party is a nice **surprise.**

T t

tale I like to read this **tale** of the wild west.

tame A **tame** dog is not mean.

tease It is not nice to **tease** people and make them cry.

tent We sleep in our **tent** in the woods.

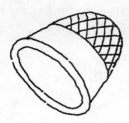

thank I **thank** you for the present.

thimble I wear a **thimble** on my thumb when I sew.

thin The **thin** log was hard to walk on.

through The mouse climbed **through** the tunnel.

throw We **throw** the ball back and forth.

thunder **Thunder** is the sound that follows lightning.

ticket You need a **ticket** to ride the train.

tiger A **tiger** is a member of the cat family.

tiny An ant is a **tiny** insect.

tip I sharpen the **tip** of my pencil.

toothbrush I like to brush my teeth with a blue **toothbrush.**

tornado A **tornado** is a storm with big winds.

tour We went on a **tour** and saw the whole town.

tractor The farmer rode a **tractor** in the field.

travel I want to **travel** to Spain one day.

tumble Penguins **tumble** and fall on the ice.

turtle My pet **turtle** has a hard, green shell.

U u

uniform The police officer wears a **uniform.**

V v

valley A **valley** is low land between hills or mountains.

W w

weed **1.** We pulled the **weed** out of the flowerbed. **2.** The farmer will **weed** his field.

west Look to the **west** to see the most beautiful sunset.

wheelbarrow Carry tools in this **wheelbarrow.**

whisper I will **whisper** the secret to you.

wicked **Wicked** people are not kind.

wide No one could jump across the **wide** river.

wigwam A **wigwam** is a house made of bark or animal skins.

wink I close one eye to **wink.**

without Do not read **without** your glasses.

Y y

yawn We watched the tired lions open their mouths and **yawn.**

A—F Word Bank

G—M Word Bank

N—S Word Bank

T—Z Word Bank